FLORIDA'S RIVERS

Cypress Spring along Holmes Creek often displays a pristine quality.

FLORIDA'S RIVERS

A CELEBRATION OF OVER 40 OF THE SUNSHINE STATE'S DYNAMIC WATERWAYS

DOUG ALDERSON

PINEAPPLE PRESS
Palm Beach, Florida

For all who enjoy and seek to protect our precious waterways

Pineapple Press, Inc.
An imprint of Globe Pequot, the trade diivision of The Rowman & Littlefield Publishing Group, Inc.
246 Goose Lane, Suite 200
Guilford, CT 06437
PineapplePress.com

British Library Cataloguing in Publication Information Available

Library of Congress Cataloging-in-Publication Data

978-1-68334-261-8 (cloth)
978-1-68334-262-5 (electronic)

♾™ The paper used in this publication meets the minimum requirements of
American National Standard for Information Sciences—Permanence of Paper for
Printed Library Materials, ANSI/NISO Z39.48-1992.

A serene section of the Hillsborough River just above the 17 Runs.

A cypress in fall on the Wacissa River.

CONTENTS

A paddler on the Wekiva River.

INTRODUCTION

There is a dreamy sense of enjoyment in floating along with the river in a wild, uninhabited region. The morning dawns slowly, and the smooth water presents a beautiful appearance, seemingly covered by a mass of white clouds, which slowly disappear as the sun rises higher and higher in the heavens. All nature is fresh and sweet after its baptism of dew, and a few remaining drops still sparkle on the leaves as they sway and rustle in the morning breeze.

—OWEN NOX, *SOUTHERN RAMBLES: FLORIDA*, 1881

Under a live oak tree on the shore one puts his cheek down against the warm earth, and looks across the sweep of yellow water; on and on the eye travels, until the great waste of multitudinous ripples is low in the sky beyond; the river pervades all space, it is supreme. It is easy to realize how a river commends itself to the necessity of the soul for worship. It calls forth adoration, as all things at once great and indifferent demand adoration. Very likely this passion for a great river, which stirs almost every man, springs from some twist in the brain left by an Aryan ancestor who prayed upon the banks of his holy river, offering his wreaths of lotus and his first-fruits of corn and wine to its majestic tide.

—MARGARET DELAND, *FLORIDA DAYS*, 1889

Meditation and water are wedded forever.

—HERMAN MELVILLE

Mother alligator with young.

Florida has long been shaped by water. Millions of years ago, as separate islands merged together to form a more solid peninsular land mass, rivers began to form. A few carved deep channels with high bluffs and banks, while others merely spread across a marshy plain. Some rivers formed because burgeoning springs needed an outlet for water to escape, while others collected excess rainfall from higher ground.

Nearly all Florida rivers, even those that mysteriously swirl underground into sinkholes, eventually spill into the Gulf of Mexico or Atlantic Ocean, continuing the cycle of water returning to water and coming back again in the form of rainfall.

For people, Florida rivers are flowing cathedrals. They are avenues through time, allowing us to wrap ourselves in a rich historical tapestry, and they are showcases for wildlife and natural beauty. Who doesn't get a thrill when watching a family of otters, or seeing a pod of manatees feeding on eelgrass, or witnessing an osprey hitting the water as it grabs a fish? These unforgettable encounters can be found along Florida rivers daily. The key is to move slowly and quietly enough to observe and listen.

On some rivers, idyllic scenes are revealed around bend after bend, appearing as they did when early native people plied the waters in dugout canoes. And rivers have many moods. They can change appearance by the hour, day, and season, with each storm and drought. You can find something new on each trip down a Florida river, even one you've visited many times before.

Florida rivers are seductive. Imagine gliding along a clear watercourse beneath a leafy canopy of maple, cypress, and gum. The current swirls eelgrass in undulating patterns as schools of silvery mullet shoot past. Ahead, a manatee's snout breaks the surface in a loud whoosh, its gray body lumbering slowly along and showing little fear as you pass by. A red-shouldered hawk cries and soars over treetops while a black anhinga stretches long wings to dry while perched on a cypress knee. This is Florida, and the scene plays out daily in the Sunshine State. Coupled with other types of rivers, such as mysterious blackwater streams and mighty alluvial ones, Florida is a paddler's and boater's paradise.

This book is a celebration of Florida's rivers, both in prose and photographs. The final chapter describes ways you can help Florida's rivers. May it inspire you to enjoy, conserve, and protect.

MIGHTY RIVERS

Mighty. That's the word that comes to mind with a handful of Florida rivers. They are the long rivers with flow and muscle, rivers that have historically been workhorses for transporting goods and people. Think Mississippi, our country's most famous river.

In Florida we have the mighty St. Johns, Apalachicola, Suwannee, Choctawhatchee, and Peace. Three of those emerge in Alabama or Georgia, and the Apalachicola is the only one with a source in the Appalachian Mountains. In fact, there is a gap on the Appalachian Trail, the Chattahoochee Gap, which crosses a tiny stream that becomes the Chattahoochee River which, in turn, joins the Flint River at the Florida border to form the Apalachicola.

For the paddler, a trip down a mighty river generally means less exertion because of the greater flow, with the exception of the slow-moving St. Johns or parts of the Peace. Sandbars can be abundant in low water, and there are numerous side streams to explore. There is also a greater chance of seeing majestic migrating fish such as gulf sturgeon, which still use some of these rivers as they did in historic times.

Fishing has always been popular along Florida's mighty rivers, but few anglers today have quite the same experience as Lamb Savage, who grew up near the St. Johns River in the late 1800s. He recalled those times in a 1953 issue of *Florida Wildlife* magazine: "We lived about five miles from the river and had to use machetes to cut through except where the narrow bridge crossed. There were Indians scattered over the area but we never had any trouble with them. . . . There wuz always plenty of fish caught in a short time and some of the boys would cut swamp cabbage. You know, that's the heart or bud of the cabbage palm. Mother cooked it like cabbage and flavored it with bacon fat" (Sarah Alberson).

Wild azalea along the Choctawhatchee River.

The Savage family made their own salt along the coast by boiling seawater in a kettle; shoes were made at home from cowhide; and medicines were made from herbs, weeds, and trees. The trail to Orlando was sandy and rutted. Times have certainly changed in the Sunshine State, but not so much when floating or fishing on one of Florida's mighty rivers. With so many miles of protected public land, the scenery is reminiscent of the time when pioneers such as Lamb Savage fished the waters, and when Native Americans plied the rivers in dugout canoes.

CHOCTAWHATCHEE

The Choctawhatchee—"River of the Choctaws"—courses into Florida from Alabama like a river on a mission. The current can be swift and sediment-laden, the river wide enough for a flotilla of watercraft side by side. Only it doesn't stay that way—the swiftness, yes—but not the width. Below U.S. Highway 90, narrow turns and sudden snags can greet the paddler or boater, depending on the water level.

On the inaugural Paddle Florida Choctawhatchee trip in 2018, nine kayakers out of sixty tipped over in this stretch. That's right, nine. One person was sent to the hospital with hypothermia courtesy of a Florida Fish and Wildlife Conservation Commission (FWC) rescue boat. On average, Paddle Florida had been doing six trips a year for almost a dozen years, but day three of the Choctawhatchee Challenge was its most dangerous moment, mainly because of the wet seasonal conditions and the fact that the river was unfamiliar to nearly everyone. Caution was the rule for the rest of the six-day trip to Highway 20.

Besides the challenges, what also struck the Paddle Florida group was the Choctawhatchee's wilderness nature. The shores showed little development, and when it did, it was mostly rustic river cabins. There were also clear first-magnitude springs that fed into the river and old-growth floodplain trees. One sharp bend a few miles above Highway 20 showed off a dozen or more massive old-growth cypress reminiscent of the days before logging ever descended upon Florida's rivers. It's no wonder some ornithologists consider the Choctawhatchee one of the last possible holdouts of the ivory-billed woodpecker, a bird almost entirely dependent on old-growth trees and largely considered extinct. It is the ghost of southern river swamps, and it especially seems to haunt the Choctawhatchee and its floodplain forests.

In 2004, when a kayaker and two bird-watchers claimed to have spotted an ivory-billed woodpecker in the Big Woods area of Arkansas, researchers began a massive search to find the species in other parts of the South. Ornithologist Dr. Geoff Hill of Auburn University and a small team of researchers first investigated Alabama's Pea River, following up on a reported sighting 10 years before. They found little in the way of potential ivory-bill habitat. Since the Pea River flowed into the larger Choctawhatchee River, which wound its way through a wide floodplain to the Gulf of Mexico, they crossed into Florida to continue their search. The Choctawhatchee was little known to ornithologists, Hill said, and for some reason, rare bird collectors around the turn of the last century had avoided the river basin.

Having poor maps of the area, the team launched their kayaks at a landing as part of an initial analysis of potential ivory-bill habitat. Within an hour, one of Hill's research assistants shockingly said he spotted an ivory-billed woodpecker in flight, while Hill heard the classic "double knock" tap normally associated with the birds. "We really never dreamed we'd actually find an ivory-bill," said Hill afterward. During subsequent studies, Hill's team claimed to have spotted ivory-billed woodpeckers on thirteen other occasions, although photographic proof was lacking.

Dr. Hill claims that the species hung on in the Choctawhatchee River basin because it was selectively logged in the past, never clear-cut in huge swaths. Ivory-billed woodpeckers prefer old-growth bottomland forests for feeding and nesting, and the Choctawhatchee basin boasts one of the largest mature swamp forests in the southeastern United States. It spans about 60 square miles, and it is relatively unpopulated by humans.

A lone kayaker on the Choctawhatchee River.

Morrison Springs.

The good news is that most of the Choctawhatchee's floodplain is now owned by the Northwest Florida Water Management District. Logging is minimal or nonexistent. The habitat will continue to mature and rejuvenate, so if ivory-bills miraculously exist, they will likely have ample habitat. To ever see one, birdwatchers would have to leave the main river channel and meticulously explore side creeks and the vast floodplain forest, places where just a few hunters venture every year.

Below Highway 20, the main Choctawhatchee channel spreads out into several braids until it flows into Choctawhatchee Bay. For experienced paddlers or boaters only, a GPS unit and good maps are recommended to tackle this section.

Camping is permitted along the river at Commanders Landing, Dead River Park Landing, and Boynton Cutoff Landing. For the upper 43 miles, however, from Highway 2 to Commanders Landing, camping is mostly limited to sandbars that may be covered during high water. The most notable springs along the river is Morrison Springs, accessible by a scenic spring run. Protected as a county park, the main spring is 250 feet in diameter, pumping out 48 million gallons of water daily. Unless the river is at flood stage and has backed up into the spring, the underwater views are spectacular and not to be missed.

On a cultural note, the Choctawhatchee River has long been home to Muscogee Creek Indians and their descendants, beginning around 1837 when Muscogee Indians ventured down the remote river from Alabama to escape forced removal to Oklahoma. The group tried to coexist with nearby settlers and hide their Indian identity the best they could. The tiny town of Bruce, Florida, on the west side of the river, is a stronghold of Muscogee descendants to this day and is the headquarters of the Muscogee Nation of Florida, which has a membership of around 400. A small museum and cultural center is open to the public.

Another Panhandle river of a similar nature is the Escambia near Pensacola. Alluvial in nature, the Escambia is 92 miles long, of which 54 miles flows through Florida. The river supports 85 native freshwater fish species—the highest variety in Florida—including the rare and endangered Gulf Coast sturgeon, saddleback darter, and cypress minnow. Other rare species include the seal salamander, Escambia map turtle, and Gulf Coast smooth softshell turtle. The river is renowned for its freshwater fishing.

Choctawatchee sunrise, cypresses, and fog.

APALACHICOLA

The drainage basin of the Apalachicola-Chattahoochee-Flint River basin is massive—more than 19,000 square miles. It begins as a trickle in the Appalachian Mountains, but by the time the Chattahoochee and Flint rivers join together at the Georgia border, the Apalachicola carries the largest water volume of any Florida river. For the paddler and boater, there are also scenic bluffs to enjoy, massive sandbars for camping and rest stops at mid- to low water levels, and lots of magnificent bird life such as bald eagles and swallow-tailed kites. Bear, deer, and turkey can sometimes be spotted along the shores in early morning, and playful otters can be seen if you're lucky.

To help ensure protection of this unique basin, the state of Florida has purchased more than 300,000 acres over the past quarter-century, and private conservation groups such as the Nature Conservancy have protected large tracts above Bristol. Altogether, with federal land holdings, nearly 750,000 acres in Florida's portion of the tristate basin is under conservation stewardship.

The river, nearing its long journey's end, spreads out like a mighty clutching hand with a dozen writhing, greedy fingers reaching for the sea. But the sea is loath to feel the muddy touch of it, and for time beyond time has been casting barriers of sand in the river's face; and always the river has overwhelmed the barriers, filling the spaces in between with alluvium and secretly hiding its work with the darkness and the silence of gum trees and tupelo and cypress. And in the ceaseless battle the river's fingers have grown ever longer and more crooked, and the black reaches of the swamps so vast that no one man is ever likely to see the whole of them.

—ALEXANDER KEY, *THE WRATH AND THE WIND*, 1949

Kayaks and Alum Bluff along the Apalachicola River.

The upper-river bluffs, the largest in Florida, are unique in another way. They were part of the original Garden of Eden, the one where Adam romped with Eve in a natural paradise until lured by Satan to bite the forbidden apple. At least that was the theory put forth by the late E. E. Callaway, former minister, NAACP (National Association for the Advancement of Colored People) lawyer, and one-time Republican nominee for governor from nearby Bristol. In his hard-to-find 1971 book, *In the Beginning*, Callaway lays out the boundaries and evidence.

Geographically, Callaway points out that the Apalachicola River is a natural waterway formed by four other rivers: the Flint, Chattahoochee, Fish Pond Creek, and Spring Creek. The original names of the rivers and land were transposed to western Asia and Africa after the Flood, he states, and "those names have had more to do with the assumption that the Garden of Eden was in western Asia than everything else."

Almost every family of fruit tree is represented in the region, from pear to fig. Even the apple—Southern crabapple to be exact—can be found in hollows and deep ravines, along the shores of gold-tinted creeks. Eve must have found the fruit tempting but extremely bitter once she took a bite. There are plenty of serpents, too, mostly northern copperheads that are regionally abundant.

Callaway maintains that the gopher wood that Noah used to build the ark was none other than the torreya tree, the rarest conifer in the world. The wood is resistant to rot, although a blight currently prevents any torreya tree in the valley from reaching maturity.

Wild theory or not, Callaway was right about one thing: "Eden means a place of delight. It suggests the choicest of all earthly places which could be inhabited by human beings."

The Apalachicola bluffs and ravines can seem Eden-like in the cool months, when biting bugs are absent and golden creeks course through a hilly, forested land that seems more like the Appalachian Mountains than Florida.

Bear tracks going to water along the Apalachicola River.

A bear track along the Apalachicola River.

The middle section of the Apalachicola is marked by sharp turns, numerous sandbars, a wider floodplain, and the river town of Wewahitchka. For more than 80 years, Donald Lanier has lived along the river near Wewahitchka. He learned the family beekeeping trade in the wide river floodplain, and he later worked on a snag boat for the Army Corps of Engineers. "My parents took me down the river in an apple crate when I was three weeks old," he said with a chuckle, "and I've been going down ever since. I put a lot of gray hairs in [my parents'] heads. I could tell you many stories."

In one story, Lanier recalled a visiting group of football players when he was a young man. Everyone stayed in the family river cabin, and it was cold that night, so Lanier went out for some wood to rekindle the stove. It was then that he saw a panther, and the cat let out a loud scream. "I hit the door hard when I came in and those football players were climbing into the rafters," he said. "They thought I was the panther."

Lanier is still saddened that thousands of acres of floodplain were sold to a paper company in the 1960s and were promptly clear-cut. "There used to be beautiful open hammocks in the floodplain and that's where we put our bees." The state of Florida has since purchased most of the floodplains and they are slowly recovering. The lower Apalachicola River basin has the largest concentration of tupelo trees in the world, although an estimated 3.7 million have died due to chronic low-water conditions over the past 20 years, and that has impacted the tupelo honey crop. "There aren't as many tupelos as there used to be," Lanier concluded.

Even in ideal conditions, producing tupelo honey is not an easy proposition. "It is a lot of trouble to bring bees downriver on a barge and set them on elevated platforms above the water level," he said. "When the tupelos start blooming, it is a pretty delicate operation."

To make pure tupelo honey, the combs must be clean just before the Ogeechee tupelo trees (white tupelo) bloom for about two weeks in late April and May, and the honey must be harvested just as the blooms fade so that no other nectar sources can contaminate the honey. Timing is critical. Plus, too much rainfall or too little rainfall, or a late frost or too much wind, can affect the tupelo blossoms and honey production. The payoff is a honey that never crystallizes. Tupelo honey is never heated, processed, or filtered in order to keep its unique ingredients pure. And Ogeechee tupelo honey has a unique composition—being high in fructose and low in glucose—that allows some diabetics to use it in small quantities as a sweetener. In short, tupelo honey is a rare breed compared to most other honeys.

Avocets in early morning along the Apalachicola.

An eagle drying its wings.

Real tupelo honey has a light golden amber hue and often a slight green cast. The flavor is distinct. It is usually more expensive than other honeys, but that reflects the effort and expertise that goes into it and the often short supply. Old-timers like Donald Lanier can tell you why, and a whole lot more.

Besides unique tupelo honey, the Apalachicola River is historically rich, evidenced by the remains of steamboats and other vintage craft seen along shores during low-water periods. Paddle wheelers and steamships once carried passengers up and down the river, the traditional voyage being from Columbus, Georgia, to Apalachicola and back. Cotton was king in the 1800s, and Apalachicola became the third-largest port along the Gulf of Mexico, shipping more than 100,000 bales a year between 1843 and 1851.

Before steamboats, Native Americans plied the waters in dugout canoes for thousands of years, and during the late 1700s and early 1800s, the river became a refuge for escaped slaves. At Prospect Bluff, the British—after losing the War of 1812—gave up a fully armed fort to Native Americans, free blacks, and escaped slaves. The occupancy was short lived,

however. Andrew Jackson sent naval and land forces into the then Spanish territory in 1815 to destroy the "Negro Fort." During a cannon battle with naval ships, a glowing-hot cannonball landed in the fort's magazine, setting off a rocking explosion that killed 270 occupants. The Americans eventually rebuilt the fort a few years later and named it Fort Gadsden after its builder. Today, it is known as the Prospect Bluff Historic Sites, managed by the U.S. Forest Service.

Below Prospect Bluff, the river widens considerably and, for the paddler, rest stops are few, and tides and winds have a larger influence. Most paddlers end their trip at Apalachicola's Battery Park on Apalachicola Bay. A seafood dinner and adult beverages are usually in order, and if you haven't spent any time in the city, it's worth a couple of days to explore more fully.

Alexander Key, author of a classic 1949 historical novel about the region, *The Wrath and the Wind*, provides a sense of history of Apalachicola's port city in this scene set in 1841:

It was very old, this place. He could feel its age in the crushed shell under his feet, the ancient shell of centuries of mollusk-eating races. It paved the streets and lay solidly under everything, a reminder that man had always lived here. Probably this spot, this remote jutting of shell and sand and alluvium and hoary trees where river and sea met, had seen continuous habitation for a thousand years. And it seemed to resent newness, for it quickly cast its cloak of age on every recent thing. It somehow gave to the present town—this young city with its sprawling new houses and lighted streets that run down to the main square and the market place along the river—a look of lazy and sedate dignity as if it had been here always.

Strolling through historic Apalachicola today is always a pleasure. First, there is the waterfront—shrimp boats, restaurants, the maritime museum, and historic buildings with a salty character. One such building

is the abandoned Taranto Seafood Company with its chutes along the side for shucked oyster shells. I first visited an Apalachicola oyster house in the late 1970s and the owner allowed me to take photos and interview some of the oyster shuckers. It was a different world that made a lasting impression.

The oyster industry has suffered in recent years due to drought and water being used and held back in Georgia by farmers, the City of Atlanta, and the Army Corps of Engineers. A water war has been raging for years with no real end in sight, but there are good people throughout the basin who continue working toward a solution.

Just up from the waterfront, Apalachicola's downtown streets are lined with antique, novelty, and clothing shops; more fine restaurants; the historic Dixie

Vintage steamship engine of the Barbara Hunt, *the last original paddle wheeler to operate on the Apalachicola, abandoned near Chattahoochee in 1940. Numerous steamships and paddle wheelers carried goods and people on the Apalachicola River in the 1800s and early 1900s.*

Theater; and the equally historic Gibson Inn. The Dixie Theater, first opened in 1912, was restored in 1998, and now hosts theater and musical productions and special events, while the Gibson Inn has been operational since 1907. My wife and I stayed at the Gibson for one of our anniversaries, and although we were forewarned by a friend that it was haunted, we slept fine.

If you want to stretch your legs, you can take the self-guided Historic Apalachicola Walking Tour. The town boasts more than 900 historic homes and buildings that were built when Apalachicola was a thriving port city. My great-grandfather jumped ship in Apalachicola around 1900, so I always like to imagine how he saw the town back then.

The town of Apalachicola is always a welcome sight at the end of a long paddling trip down the river. I've paddled the entire 107-mile river several times as part of the annual October Apalachicola RiverTrek, a fundraiser and educational five-day trip sponsored by Apalachicola Riverkeeper. For five days, participants paddle, swim, play, camp, and learn about the river and its rich floodplain from scientists and longtime river residents. There is no better way to get to know the river and its challenges, and to develop a community of dedicated river advocates.

Apalachicola Riverkeeper hosts a web page consisting of maps and a data book created in partnership with the Florida Office of Greenways and Trails so that people can plan trips on the river, whether for a few miles or several days. Fall and early winter is an ideal time to paddle the Apalachicola because the river is low enough to expose numerous sandbars for camping and rest stops. The river can be at flood stage in spring, making it problematic for overnight trips. The Blueway Guide provides suggested water levels based on river gauges that can be accessed online. At moderate to low water levels, more sandbars are exposed for camping and frequent swim breaks to keep spirits high and muscles relaxed.

Apalachicola Side Streams

Besides the main river, the Apalachicola basin has enough side streams to keep a paddler or boater busy for weeks. One mapped system is the 100-mile Apalachicola River Paddling Trail System along the lower river and bay. With intriguing names such as Thank You Ma'am Creek and Whiskey George, these are mostly short, easy trails that meander through tupelo and cypress swamps; many lead to open bays. There

Devon Creek canopy off the Apalachicola River.

Reflections on Graham Creek, one of the river's many tributaries.

are some designated campsites if you want to plan a multiday trip.

Graham Creek is one of my favorites. If you drive on Highway 65 about 10 miles south of Sumatra, you'll cross over it, and there is easy access near the southwest corner of the bridge.

The blackwater creek is perfect to explore by kayak, canoe, or paddleboard and good for beginners. If you follow the waterway east, you can paddle a couple of miles into the famed (or infamous) Tate's Hell Swamp. Here, the waterway gradually narrows through a maze of cypress and tupelo trees with their swollen bases and myriad trunks. Some have been storm-battered and scarred by lightning, but they remain alive. Thick overhead branches eventually form an interlocking canopy. The obsidian-black water is usually still because current is virtually absent. It's like paddling through a mirror.

Only an occasional fish or alligator breaks the stillness. Yes, there are some gators, but they are normally shy and quietly sink to the bottom as a paddler or boater approaches. You can follow their bubbles!

The creek widens on the west side of the Highway 65 bridge, but several side creeks offer a more intimate experience beneath tree canopies. Along one tributary about a quarter-mile west of the bridge, a giant cypress with a twisted base resembles the head of a mastodon, depending on the angle and water height.

Other weathered cypress trees along this waterway have been riddled by woodpeckers. Some holes were likely made by ivory-billed woodpeckers decades ago. It's a reminder of how the past seems to merge with the present in this wild place called Graham Creek.

Fall is a popular time to visit these river swamps since cypress needles turn gold and copper colored and tupelo leaves blaze yellow and orange. Late April or May is another ideal time since the tupelo trees may be blooming and the drone of honeybees fills the air. Prothonotary warblers often can be spotted, bright yellow against the gray tree trunks and branches. This is our only cavity nesting warbler, and it prefers cypress and gum swamps and hardwood bottomlands.

Florida's mighty Apalachicola and its many tributaries are beautiful and dynamic and worthy of exploration.

Morning along the Suwannee River, just below Suwannee Springs.

SUWANNEE

The Suwannee is a hybrid river that defies categorization. During normal water level, it is a tannin waterway fed by both the vast Okefenokee Swamp—one of the Southeast's largest wetlands—and numerous springs. In fact, the Suwannee basin is believed to have the largest concentration of freshwater springs in the world, and during severe droughts, the river flow consists almost entirely of clear springwater. During high water or flood stage, the springs are usually inundated and can actually reverse flow, taking in river water instead of pumping out groundwater. During these times, the river carries large volumes of sediments, so it takes on alluvial characteristics.

The Suwannee at low water is perhaps the most scenic, with numerous limestone bluffs and even small caves visible in places. Shoals that are normally inundated, such as below Ellaville, can produce excitement for paddlers and boaters, and the springs alongside the river have the best clarity. The current can be sluggish,

Having supplied ourselves with ammunition and provision, we set off in the cool of the morning, and descended pleasantly, riding on the crystal flood, which flows down with an easy, gentle, yet active current, rolling over its silvery bed. The stream almost as transparent as the air we breathe; there is nothing done in secret except on its green flowery verges.

—WILLIAM BARTRAM, 1773, COMMENTING ON A CLEAR SUWANNEE RIVER

Big Shoals on the Suwannee River in springtime at low to moderate water levels.

however, and there might be sandbars just under the surface that can temporarily halt forward progress.

In springtime, Big Shoals just above White Springs is often at the ideal water level to test your skills at running Florida's largest whitewater rapids. The river drops nine feet in a quarter-mile. When the river gauge is between 55 and 61 feet at White Springs, Big Shoals is the Sunshine State's only class-three rapids. A good portage trail runs alongside the shoals for those not willing to attempt it or when water levels are too low.

The beauty of the Suwannee for paddlers is that it has everything—wild beauty, history, shoals, springs, and free river camps. Yes, you can stay for free in screened pavilions with ceiling fans with access to restrooms and hot showers. Nowhere else in the state can you get such a deal. There are five river camps only accessible from the water and, in some cases, by hiking trail; these were designed by state and local partners to promote ecotourism and to reduce the impacts of shoreline camping. In places where there are no river camps, you can access state parks or private campgrounds or camp in riverside parks such as in Branford. The Suwannee is usually on every new paddler's bucket list, and is ideally suited for multiday trips.

Before any trip down the Suwannee, seek to grasp some of the river's storied history because reminders of the past are still visible in key locations. The river is a meandering history museum, the Suwannee being a busier place in the past than it is today.

Small wood-burning sternwheelers once shipped cotton, tobacco, peanuts, naval stores, lumber, and cedar logs on the river. The queen of the fleet was the *Belle of the Suwannee,* captained by Robert Bartlett. Another boat, the *Madison,* carried mail and served as a floating trading post during a time when roads were sometimes impassable. During the Civil War, Confederates converted the boat into a makeshift gunboat but eventually scuttled it in Troy Spring lest it fall into Union hands. The lower ribs, keel, and metal spikes of the ship are still visible in the spring run, so make sure you bring a mask and snorkel when visiting Troy Spring and the river's many other springs.

Big Shoals in springtime at the ideal water level for class-three rapids, the only one of its kind in Florida.

A vibrant tourism industry once centered around the Suwannee's many mineral springs. White Sulphur Springs was the first Florida mineral spring to be commercialized, initially featured as Jackson Springs in 1831. A log cabin springhouse was built, followed by a concrete-and-coquina structure in 1903. The spring attraction gave rise to the town, and by the 1880s visitors could choose from 500 hotel and boardinghouse rooms. Today, White Springs is a mere shell of its former vitality, although one can visit the reconstructed springhouse, minus the sitting platforms.

When floating past White Springs, the carillon bell tower in Stephen Foster Folk Culture Center State Park plays Foster's popular tunes, especially his 1851 *Way Down Upon the Suwannee River,* even though the songwriter never cast eyes on the waterway. It is one reason author Cecile Hulse Matschat wrote in *Suwannee River: Strange Green Land* in 1938: "Of all the rivers in America the Suwannee is the most romantic. It has a place beside the royal rivers of the world, though no New York, Paris, or London sprawls along its banks, and no torrential cataract appears in its course to challenge Niagara."

Downstream from White Springs, Suwannee Springs was once a major health resort from the Civil War to the 1920s. The spring area had a succession of four hotels, a bathhouse, and several cottages. A spur line along the Savannah, Florida & Western Railway brought thousands of visitors annually, lured by promises of healing waters that could cure everything from kidney troubles to nervous prostration. The resort faded with the railroad, and the last hotel burned in 1925. Only ruins of the complex remain, but the springs itself is now public property. Visitors can swim inside the original stone walls of the bathhouse and discover for themselves if the springwater, which smells like a lost Easter egg, can cure what ails them.

As water from Suwannee Springs enters the river, it resembles Jacob Rhett (J. R.) Motte's account in the winter of 1836 as a surgeon in the Second Seminole War:

> The Suwannee Mineral Springs is a remarkable sight; it issues from the Eastern bank of the Suwannee; the spring and the river mingling their waters together and imparting to that of the river its yellow colour half way across and a considerable distance down-

stream, and depositing upon all the surrounding rocks Sulphur in sufficient quantity to make their yellow colour apparent at a great distance.

A smattering of other springs bubble forth in this upper half of the river, and there are also rapids at certain water levels other than Big Shoals. In 1881, author Kirk Munroe began a 1,600-mile journey in a 14-foot sailing canoe at Ellaville, just below the confluence of the Withlacoochee River. Almost immediately, he encountered trouble. "Left Ellaville at 7 o'clock, rainy and thick fog," he began in his journal. "Canoe very deeply laden. A mile below town ran three rapids—foundered in second, had to jump overboard to save canoe from upset. Shipped considerable water and got blankets wet. Went into camp five miles down Suwannee River on left bank. Sun came out and I hung everything out to dry. Stayed quietly in camp all day. Very wild country and have not seen a human being either on river or shore" (see "A Lost 'Psyche'," Irving

Leonard (ed.). Munroe finished the Suwannee portion of his journey without further incident, replenishing supplies by purchasing milk and sweet potatoes from river residents and hunting squirrels.

Several rivers flow into the Suwannee in the upper reaches—the Alapaha and Withlacoochee. The Withlacoochee—often confused with the river by the same name in central Florida that flows into the Gulf—has springs and also shoals at the right water levels. The Alapaha, on the other hand, swirls underground in dramatic fashion only to emerge again just before meeting the Suwannee. Another major tributary is the Santa Fe River, described in more detail in the spring-fed rivers section.

Near Branford, the Suwannee becomes broader and large springs are more numerous. They make an already picturesque river seem like a many-jeweled necklace. About 260 freshwater springs dot the Suwannee River basin, pumping more than 2.8 billion gallons of water a day. Dubbed the Springs Heartland, it is one

The ribs of a sunken Confederate ship, the Madison, *in the spring run of Troy Spring.*

of the largest concentrations of freshwater springs in the world. They are ideal cooling-off spots when paddling in warm weather.

Just below Fanning Springs along Highway 19, the Suwannee passes the largest remaining unaltered tract of hardwood forest in the Suwannee River basin. It is part of the 3,500-acre Andrews Wildlife Management Area. Early loggers mainly focused on the area's virgin cypress and floated the logs to sawmills via the river highway, leaving other old-growth species untouched in the Andrews tract.

From the virgin hardwood forest, the Suwannee makes its way past the final large spring along the river—Manatee Springs. This region was home to the Seminole village of Talahasochte, one that William Bartram visited in 1773. Bartram provided a detailed glimpse of early Seminole life, and he was especially impressed with their canoes. "These Indians have large handsome canoes, which they form out of the trunks of cypress trees (*Cupressus disticha*), some of them commodious enough to accommodate twenty or thirty warriors," he wrote. "In those large canoes they descend the river on trading and hunting expeditions to the sea coast, neighboring islands and keys, quite to the point of Florida, and sometimes cross the Gulf, extending their navigations to the Bahama islands and even to Cuba: a crew of the adventurers had just arrived, having returned from Cuba but a few days before our arrival, with a cargo of spirituous liquors, Coffee, Sugar, and Tobacco." In return, the Seminoles traded deerskins, furs, dried fish, beeswax, honey, bear's oil, and other items.

The downfall of the Seminoles along the Suwannee began in 1818 when Andrew Jackson and a huge force of regulars, Tennessee volunteers, Georgia militia, and Creek Indian allies attacked villages of Indians and escaped slaves downstream at Old Town. The Seminoles dispersed but eventually returned, prompting the building of Fort Fanning near Fanning Springs during the Second Seminole War in 1838. The fort guarded a key river crossing and was a base for operations to clear out Seminoles in the region. Most Indians were eventually deported to Oklahoma while a small band ultimately survived in a swamp even deeper and wilder than Okefenokee—the Everglades.

After Manatee Springs, the Suwannee makes its final run to the Gulf of Mexico, passing through the Lower Suwannee National Wildlife Refuge. The wide river mouth boasts expansive watery vistas, marsh-lined tidal creeks, and small tree-covered islands. This is where the Suwannee releases freshwater and nutrients—its lifeblood—to a hungry Gulf. In return, the river takes in mullet, sturgeon, manatee, and a host of other aquatic lifeforms. The Suwannee provides cold-weather sanctuary for these creatures along with spawning and feeding areas.

Evening along the Suwannee River at Suwannee River State Park.

Reflections and mossy boulders at Manatee Springs.

It is an age-old exchange unaffected by man-made dams or structures.

This lower Suwannee region boasts a rich pirate history, as described by the Florida Writer's Project in 1939:

> In the early 1780's pirate craft made their rendezvous among the secluded inlets and bays of Suwannee Sound; tales of murder and buried treasure persist to this day. Expeditions have been outfitted, stock companies organized, and countless excavations made to recover hidden stores of gold, the whereabouts of which have been learned, as convention requires, from old maps, or the lips of dying sailors; no successful quests have been recorded, however.

In order to protect the Suwannee's many unique qualities, the Suwannee River Water Management District has been purchasing land and development rights from willing landowners. Plus, several state and local parks have been added in the past quarter-century. It is an impressive feat when considering Florida's conservation history of the 1970s, when local opposition defeated several federal attempts to protect the Suwannee through the national wild and scenic rivers program. The land purchases are helping to protect the river and make any river journey more enjoyable.

Suwannee Water
Touching the Suwannee
I feel her many springs
Her cypress and limestone
Shoals and high banks.
Touching the Suwannee
I sense her rich history
Dugouts and river boats
Mineral spas and bluegrass.
Touching the Suwannee
I know her troubles
And wonder what people will feel
When they touch the Suwannee
A century from now.

ST. JOHNS

If the St. Johns River were a mammal, a three-toed sloth would size it up pretty well. The river drops only 27 feet over its entire 310-mile course. Twenty-seven feet! A mountain river such as the Chattooga drops an average of 49 feet per mile, so one will not encounter whitewater rapids on the St. Johns River. In fact, tidal influences can actually reverse the river's flow 161 miles upstream from its mouth during drought periods.

Despite its gentle and sometimes nonexistent current, boating on the St. Johns River is not without risk. Margaret Deland, writing in *Florida Days* in 1889, lures one in with her sweeping prose about the mighty St. Johns River before gently offering an ominous warning:

> The yellow current of the St. Johns River lies against the sky in a great curve towards the north; the farther shore is so low and flat and dim, in the flooding light, that it seems but a bank of mist, faintly golden in the sunshine.

If I could have, to hold forever, one brief place and time of beauty, I think I might choose the night on that high lonely bank above the St. Johns River.

—MARJORIE KINNAN RAWLINGS, *CROSS CREEK*

Neither the Mississippi nor the Nile exceeds the average expanse of the St. Johns between shore to shore for a full hundred miles above its mouth; and with corpulence, you would say, it combines laziness. Indeed, the fact that this river's gleaming, broad surface so much more frequently resembles the superficies of a lake than a moving current very long ago led the adjacent Indians to call the St. Johns "Welaka"—which meant The Chain of Lakes.

—BRANCH CABELL AND A. J. HANNA, *THE ST. JOHNS: A PARADE OF DIVERSITIES*

G 5672 At the Wharf, Palatka, Fla.

Postcard of a steamboat at Palatka on the St. Johns River, circa 1905. Between 1830 and 1920, about 300 paddle wheelers plied the waters of the St. Johns. ROTOGRAPH CO., NEW YORK, MADE IN GERMANY

The sweep of the current is slow and grave, so that, apparently, there is a curious fixity and permanence about it; it is without the hurry and noise of the little running rivers of the north, and it has none of their lighthearted intimacy, which comes from the crowding nearness of their trees and meadows. Not that the great river is cruel—like the ocean, or the sky, or a force in Nature. It bears a canoe as lightly and gently on its broad, smooth bosom as the most tranquil little pool might do, lying like a jewel at the feet of guarding hills; but if by some bit of carelessness, or confidence, a man trusts his life to it, it drowns him with smiling ease, and without the slightest effort to save him.

The main reason the St. Johns can be dangerous for the boater is its width in many places, especially its large lakes, leaving one vulnerable to high winds and storms. This was never more apparent than when I volunteered to help Paddle Florida on its first and only Bartram History Paddle on the famed river in 2015, the 250th anniversary of John and William Bartram's first visit to Florida in 1765. As we reached the mouth of the five-mile Salt Springs Run and gaped at the massive Lake George, most of the group understandably took a U-turn. Winds howled, and the lake's surface was a washing machine of choppiness. Only eight out of forty-five ventured forth to cross part of the lake and

A paddler on Lake George, with a storm approaching.

Georgia Boys Fish Camp along Dunn's Creek, just off the St. Johns River.

continue north. We had to work mightily just to make any progress forward. "It could be worse, it could be raining!" I yelled to a companion over the wind, quoting from the classic comedy *Young Frankenstein*. Within minutes, a squall moved toward u, and we were soon pelted with stinging rain.

After a few more miles, we finally reached our destination—Renegades on the River—a modern-style fish camp with tiki bar, live band, and restaurant. William Bartram used the river to access trading posts and Seminole Indian villages; he failed to mention tiki bars. However, our day's rough voyage was reminiscent of Bartram's 1774 visit when he encountered harsh conditions while crossing Lake George. "Now as we approach the capes, behold the little ocean of Lake George, the distant circular coast gradually rising to view, from his misty fringed horizon," he wrote in *Travels*. "I cannot entirely suppress my apprehensions of danger. My vessel at once diminished to a nut-shell

on the swelling seas, and at the distance of a few miles, must appear to the surprised observer as some aquatic animal, at intervals emerging from its surface."

The Bartram Trail in Putnam County was conceived by two citizen volunteers, Sam Carr and Dean Campbell, who sought to highlight the rich history and also to "get people onto the St. Johns River to make a personal connection with it."

The St. Johns is rich in human history, from pyramidal Native American temple mounds to early European trading posts, and the writings of John and William Bartram—father and son respectively—help to bring it to life. One site along the trail is Satsuma Springs just past the town of Welaka. The clear sulfur spring has changed little since Bartram's day, and John Bartram's 1765 description of it still rings true: "We came down a steep hill 20 foot high and about 4 or 500 yards from the river, under the foot of which issued out a large fountain (big enough to turn a mill) of warm

Dawn at Dunn's Creek State Park near the St. Johns River.

clear water of a very offensive taste, and smell like bilge-water, or the washings of a gun-barrel; the sediment that adhered to the trees fallen therein looked of a pale white or bluish cast, like milk and water mixed."

Mineral springs in Florida have long been used for healing. A large live oak near the spring is bent over to the ground, forming an arch over the access trail. Some theorize that Native Americans bent the tree when it was very young, marking the spring site to make it more visible from the water.

North of Satsuma Spring for several miles, the eastern shoreline is largely developed with riverfront homes, cabins, and fish camps, while the western shore is undeveloped, being part of the Ocala National Forest. In William Bartram's day, the western shore was where the Seminoles lived, while Spanish and English settlers occupied the eastern shore. William Bartram wrote several passages about an Indian trading post along the western shore, Spalding's Lower Store, with the funniest episode being when some Seminoles tapped into 20 kegs of rum: They were prevailed on to broach their beloved nectar; which in the end caused some disturbance, and the consumption of most of their liquor; for after they had once got a smack of it, they never were sober for ten days, and by that time there was but little left."

The nearest thing to trading posts today are fish camps such as Georgia Boys on Dunn's Creek, a river tributary. Georgia Boys, one of the oldest fish camps in the state, features about 200 handmade signs hung from the rafters and nailed to posts and walls. Some words of wisdom are worth repeating: "No wife has shot her husband while he was washing dishes." Another reads, "The difference between genius and stupidity is genius has its limits."

The St. Johns significantly widens around Palatka, once a thriving Seminole village and later a steamboat town. Now, it is an emerging trail town known for paddling and bike trails. Palatka was a thriving Seminole village when William Bartram visited: "There were eight or ten habitations, in a row; or street, fronting the water, and about fifty yards distance from it. Some of the youth were naked, up to their hips in the water, fishing with rods and lines; whilst others, younger, were diverting themselves in shooting frogs with bows and arrows. On my near approach, their little children took to their heels, and ran to some women who were hoeing corn; but the stouter youth stood their ground, and, smiling called to me."

The St. Johns River, Florida's longest at 310 miles, has multiple personalities. The headwaters area is a

Above: Kayaks at dawn at Dunn's Creek State Park.
Below: Kingfisher with fish at Blue Spring State Park along the St. Johns River. Kingfishers can be found along most of Florida's rivers.

A paddler on the upper St. Johns River.

broad marsh in Indian River County, the river flowing through an appropriately named Puzzle Lake where multiple channels make for a confusing maze. From there the river continues its famous northward journey, gradually developing a clearly defined channel and flowing through several broad lakes in the middle basin. By the time the St. Johns River reaches Palatka for its final 80-mile leg to the Atlantic Ocean, the average width is more than two miles. Not bad for a river believed to be only 5,000 to 7,500 years old in its current form.

The St. Johns River basin covers a massive 8,840 square miles, making for diverse river ecosystems that are home to hundreds of plant and animal species. These include saltwater species such as dolphins, manatees, and numerous fish species from the common redfish and flounder to the more unusual sea robin. Shrimping is common on the lower river during certain seasons, and sharks venture up the river, too—mostly harmless ones like the bonnethead, nurse, and lemon.

Given the growing human population in the St. Johns basin—about 3.5 million people and counting—along with sprawling agricultural lands, it is not surprising that pollution and water withdrawal issues pose significant challenges.

PEACE

Serene and generally slow-moving, the Peace River—known as "Rio de la Paz" on old Spanish charts—emerges from the Green Swamp and flows more than 100 miles past largely undeveloped shorelines. Calusa Indians once utilized the waterway in large numbers, especially the lower stretches near where the river meets the Gulf, and Seminole Indians called the river home in the 1700s and early 1800s. They named the river Tallackchopo, "river of long peas," after the wild peas that were abundant along the riverbanks.

Numerous creeks such as Saddle Creek, Paynes Creek, Joshua Creek, Shell Creek, and Horse Creek feed the Peace River. High banks, islands, and stately live oaks make for outstanding scenery around each bend. Considered more of a blackwater river than its alluvial cousins in the Panhandle, the Peace River is nonetheless one of Florida's major rivers in terms of history and ecology. Its basin is known as the Peace River Valley, one that covers 2,300 square miles.

Fossils are what draw many to the Peace River. After obtaining an inexpensive state permit, fossil hunters scan the shorelines and river bottom below Wachula, searching for ancient shark teeth and the bones of prehistoric animals such as dugongs, an ancestor of the

The history of the Peace River Valley of Florida in the nineteenth century is a tale of violence, passion, struggle, sacrifice, and determination. It was written with the lives and deaths of Creeks and Seminoles who refused to surrender their independence; of runaway slaves and fierce black warriors; of white frontiersmen struggling to build a better world for themselves and their families; of men and women who supported the Confederacy and their brothers and sisters who would not abandon the Union; of settlers from the defeated South and, later, from the North and Midwest; and of freedmen and women who suffered to overcome the shackles of slavery, who farmed, who built the railroads, and who toiled in the broiling heat of open-pit phosphate mines.

—CANTER BROWN, JR., *FLORIDA'S PEACE RIVER FRONTIER*

Paddling the Peace River at sunset.

Fossilized dugong rib bones along the Peace River. Dugongs were ancestors of the West Indian manatee.

Postcard, postmarked 1909, of a lower Peace River scene. A. J. BOSSELMAN & CO., NEW YORK, MADE IN GERMANY

West Indian manatee. A prized find is a megalo-
don shark tooth which can exceed five inches in
length. These marine creatures date back to the
Miocene Epoch, 5 million to 26.5 million years
ago when Florida was under water. But it was
this oceanic past that would ultimately impact
the Peace River more than anything else.

In 1881, Captain J. Francis LeBaron discovered rich deposits of phosphate near Arcadia,
phosphate being an essential component of fertilizer. Phosphate was formed millions of years
ago when the dissolved phosphorous in seawater solidified and combined with the remains of
marine animals and plants. Several phosphate
mines sprung up soon after the mineral was
discovered, with men using picks and shovels,
and even the bed of the Peace River was mined.
Today, the ribs of early wooden barges that
once carried phosphate still line the shores in
the middle river.

As mining grew in scale and became mecha-
nized, the area's water table was impacted,
causing the upper river to dry up at times. In
1950, mining was also responsible for drying up
Kessingen Spring, a popular swimming hole in
Polk County near Bartow. Today, the spring
simply resembles a shallow, dry sinkhole. Mine
restoration efforts may help to restore some of
the water flow to the Peace River, and some
dream of one day recovering Kessingen Spring.

After its long journey, the Peace River empties into the massive Charlotte Harbor where it
mingles with Gulf waters and the Myakka and
Caloosahatchee Rivers. Author Canter Brown
Jr., who wrote a comprehensive history of
the river, sums up its current appearance and
condition:

> For much of its length, Peace River passes
> through a portion of Florida still rural, and
> even remote, late in the twentieth century.
> In its upper reaches the land is scarred by
> huge open pit phosphate mines, while far-
> ther to the south cattle still graze on the
> prairies through which it flows. No great
> metropolises line the river's banks and no
> commerce passes along its waters, but once,
> less than two centuries ago, the Peace River
> witnessed events that brought the dynamics
> of history into play in South Florida, and the
> Peace River bent and molded those events
> into this story.

Island scene on the tranquil Peace River.

Whatever the distractions and distortions around them—however strip-zoned and ugly the road there might be, and however concreted and constrained those once sandy banks might have become—springs still can deliver a living piece of Florida that performs much the same way it did during our childhood, and even before that.

—AL BURT

SPRING-FED GEMS

2

Primarily found in north-central Florida and the Panhandle, spring-fed streams are largely fed by deep springs that emerge from permeable limestone layers of the vast Floridan Aquifer. Because the waters are normally clear and cool, they are extremely popular, especially in summer. Paddling, swimming, snorkeling, tubing, and wildlife viewing are major activities that occur on spring-fed streams, and Florida has more examples than any state in the nation and the world.

Florida's 700 springs pump more than 8 billion gallons of fresh water a day. The springs are ranked from one to eight depending on how much water they pump. Thirty-three of those springs, such as Wakulla, Silver, Rainbow, and Weeki Wachee, are considered first magnitude, and most of these form rivers. To prevent any one of these rivers from being loved to death, recreational use of some of the more popular spring-fed streams is becoming more regulated in hopes that their crystalline beauty can be ensured for future generations.

Many of Florida's smaller springs are accessed by side streams along larger rivers. These many side streams are often where the water is "skinny," and you might need to pull over a log or three. But these are the wild places where you will most likely spot wildlife if quiet and observant—gators, otters, turtles, owls, wood ducks . . . these places are part of Florida's magic because Florida is a water state and water can transport us to beauty and enjoyment.

The clear "Emerald Cut" of the upper Rock Springs Run near Orlando.

Above: The common gallinule, or "water chicken," is a bird frequently seen along Florida's spring-fed rivers. These three gallinule chicks were seen in midsummer along the Wakulla River with their mother close by.
Below: A coyote swims across a side stream along the Wacissa River.

COLDWATER CREEK

The name of this waterway provides a clue to its spring-fed nature. Mostly shallow and always pleasantly cool, the creek is narrow in spots with a steep gradient, providing some of the swiftest water in the state. Flowing for nearly 20 miles, primarily through the Blackwater State Forest, the shores are undeveloped and scenic. The sandy bottom and broad sandbars are reminiscent of nearby Gulf Coast beaches. It is no wonder the river is popular with both tubers and paddlers, and the brisk downstream current makes for an easy trip. Sporadic obstructions include cypress knees, logs, and wide gravel bars that extend into the stream from shorelines.

HOLMES CREEK

Perhaps every river has at least one person who knows its many moods, who can tell you if it's running high or low, who knows when the bream are bedding or the mullet are running, who knows if there's a threat or if the water quality has been impacted in some way. I met such a man on the Panhandle's Holmes Creek, a rural spring-fed stream that runs 56 miles from the Alabama border to the Choctawhatchee River. He was gray-haired and big-bellied, standing at a landing holding a beer as I landed my kayak.

"Say, are those kayaks more stable than a canoe?" he asked, nodding toward my sit-in kayak.

"They can be," I replied, "because you're closer to the water. All depends on what kind of kayak you get."

"I'd like to get me one for fishing," he said.

"You care to try mine?"

"No!" he said emphatically. "I'm too big for that thing."

I suggested he check out a sit-on-top kayak with rod holders. We then started talking about the creek. Based upon my four-hour paddling trip upstream, Holmes Creek appeared pristine, with abundant wildlife and fish. But this man claimed it had been degraded. "Used to be a lot more fish in this river," he said. "That's 'cause we'd get a lot more rain. Those fish would breed in the swamps and bays along the river and the rain would flush them out, but we don't get so many anymore. Plus, there's more people, and people have

Winter scene on Holmes Creek near Vernon.

logged nearby, causing erosion, and they've dumped stuff into the water. This river ain't what it used to be."

He was a backwoods John Muir. It pays to listen and learn.

Fed by three major springs, some of the creek's upper reaches are too swampy, shallow, and snag-ridden to be passable by boat or kayak, but the section below Cypress Spring is part of a state-designated paddling trail and usually open. Cypress Spring is one of the clearest and bluest springs in the state, relatively unmarred because the area is largely undeveloped. The nearest town is Vernon, population of less than 700.

Generally clear and canopied, the creek is a paddler's delight, and there are numerous access points to plan trips of various lengths. And just below where the creek spills into the wide Choctawhatchee is a major summer congregation area for the Gulf sturgeon, a federally protected species that is often seen leaping dramatically from the water.

ECONFINA CREEK

The key to protecting waterways is to preserve more than just the shorelines. The watersheds need protection as well, and Econfina Creek is a good example of preservation at its finest. In the 1990s, the Northwest Florida Water Management District began purchasing the Econfina watershed.

Driving the project's strong preservation and conservation measures is the fact that the Econfina provides the lion's share of water to Deer Point Lake Reservoir, the primary drinking-water source for the Gulf Coast town of Panama City and surrounding environs. It is also a critical freshwater source for St. Andrews Bay, a vital nursery for marine life. Hydrologic testing found that almost 29,000 acres of sand hills west of the creek make up a major aquifer recharge area for several high-magnitude springs that feed this vibrant watercourse.

Fortunately, the Water Management District was able to purchase most of this land from Rosewood Timber Company (Hunt Petroleum/Prosper Energy) of Houston for a little under $802 per acre in the 1990s. George Fisher, retired senior planner for the district, was instrumental in the purchase. "It was a good price," he said, "but our future cost of restoring the uplands will be pretty heavy because they had been through a couple of timber cycles of sand pines; native vegetation was pretty much destroyed. Trying to re-establish it will really be a job."

To gain a better understanding of what the recovering uplands of the Econfina will one day look like, I took a stroll on the Florida Trail just west of the river. I first walked through a thick sand pine forest that had been planted by the previous owner. Then, through the trees, I could see what appeared to be golden prairie grass. Moving closer, I realized that the "prairie" was a

Youths jump into one of Econfina Creek's many clear springs.

rolling hillside of feathery wiregrass in seed, the result of prescribed burning during the previous summer.

Wiregrass in seed can be three times taller than wiregrass that is not in seed. Scattered throughout the area were tall longleaf pines about a half-century in age, one of the few remnant maturing longleaf tracts that the district was able to purchase. I was viewing the future of thousands of acres of young longleaf forest in the Econfina Creek Water Management Area. The recovering tracts will one day resemble "a prairie with trees," a description given by early pioneers who drove wagons through the vast, parklike expanses of longleaf forests.

Another unique environment found at Econfina is steephead ravines. Steepheads are like three-sided box

canyons up to 100 feet deep that have small seepage springs and clear streams at the bottom. Steepheads erode from the bottom up as groundwater seeps through porous sand and leaks from an exposed slope. The sand above collapses and is carried away by the stream, so steepheads are continually cutting into the sandhill uplands. Since these shady wet environments are generally 10 to 15 degrees cooler than the dry uplands, steepheads harbor a unique array of plants and animals, including rare salamanders that often reside beneath mossy rocks and logs.

Besides obvious water supply/recharge, ecological, and recreational values, the Econfina Creek lands are valuable from a historical perspective. Early Native Americans lived there for millennia, from mastodon-hunting Paleo Indians to Muscogee Creek bands that moved in from Alabama and Georgia in the eighteenth and nineteenth centuries and whose descendants still remain.

Early white settlers established a wagon trail through the hilly creek land, prompting one early observer to label the area "the mountains of Florida." Perhaps the best-known early pioneer was William Gainer. He settled along a group of large emerald springs that feed the river near present-day Highway 20; the springs bear his name.

Gainer had been a scout and engineer for Andrew Jackson during his invasion of West Florida in 1818 and liked what he saw during the incursion. "This is a beautiful and productive place with great potential," he wrote to relatives in North Carolina soon after settling. "Tell our relatives and any close friends about it, but no one else." Gainer established a thriving plantation along the river, raising cotton, cattle, and other farm products.

Eventually, large moonshine stills were pumping out white lightning along Econfina Creek and Deer Point Lake, a trade that was passed down through generations. As late as 1959, the average moonshine operation was believed to be producing 60 barrels a week.

A few years ago, while canoeing the calmer middle portion of the river one summer, I ran into Martha Barnes, a graying matriarch who had pioneer ancestors buried in a nearby cemetery. She was visiting one of the river's 11 clear azure springs. "I've been coming here since I was a kid," she said. "We used to play Tarzan and swing off the vines. There was no Highway 20 then; we used to come up on dirt roads. I bring my grandkids here now. I love the fact that it will remain wild and undeveloped."

CHIPOLA

The Chipola is one of those rivers that has a bit of everything—springs, bluffs, caves, and mystery. Take the stretch where a defunct iron bridge crosses the river a few miles north of U.S. Highway 90 near County Road 162. The Bellamy Bridge—"Florida's most haunted bridge"—can be reached by hiking a half-mile through an unspoiled floodplain forest.

The site has been used as a crossing spot for centuries, and ghost stories abound, such as one about a headless wagon driver, a nineteenth-century moonshine-related murder victim, and the unsettled spirit of Elizabeth Jane Croom Bellamy, who died nearby of malaria in 1837. Hike the short access trail around sunset when the thick forest is darkening, cicadas begin whirring in treetops, barred owls start calling across the water, and a cold chill permeates the air . . .

Below Bellamy Bridge at Christoff Landing, you can paddle four and a half miles to Florida Caverns State Park on a winding, canopied river that has numerous side springs, the largest being Baltzell Spring. County workers and state park rangers periodically try to clear snags in this section, but changing water levels and storm events—especially hurricanes such as Hurricane Michael in 2018—can produce snags that may require some negotiating. This section is wild and scenic, with only a couple of houses. Florida Caverns is the only state park in Florida to offer dry cave tours, although occasionally the caves are closed during wet seasons due to partial flooding.

In the state park, the Chipola River disappears into a submerged cave for a quarter-mile before reemerging on the surface, so the next access point is the Yancey Bridge below the state park. On river right, about four miles down, the Ovens is a shallow cave at the base of a small bluff, the most consistently dry cave along a Florida river. Small side pockets off the main tunnel are reminiscent of clay ovens. Just deep enough to need a flashlight to explore, one might think the half-submerged boulders around the cave entrance were part of a Neolithic monument.

Just over a mile below the Ovens on river left is a narrow spring run that leads to Maund Spring, a lovely spot for a swim and a picnic. Another good stopping point is the wider Spring Creek a couple of miles below on river left. The ever-clear Spring Creek is fed by several springs in the Merritt's Mill Pond just north of U.S. Highway 90. Numerous tubers float down Spring Creek during the summer months.

Facing page: Econfina Creek is slowly recovering from damage caused by Hurricane Michael in 2018.

Below the State Road 274 Bridge above Lamb Eddy Park, paddlers and boaters have fun running several shoals, including "Look-N-Tremble Falls," a class-one rapids. At times, people joke and call this the "Look-N-Giggle Falls," but the shoals can vary in difficulty depending on the water level. Scouting is suggested. If the water is too low, portaging is advised since the limestone rocks can bang up your boat.

The river winds through an impressive cypress forest just above Scott's Ferry, and special care should be taken to follow the main channel. Below Scott's Ferry, the river enters the ethereal-looking Dead Lakes area. Dead Lakes was initially formed by natural sandbars along the Apalachicola River that backed up the river and caused many of the cypress trees to perish. Camping is permitted at the county-run Dead Lakes Park in Wewahitchka. A GPS unit is recommended for navigating in the Dead Lakes.

From the Dead Lakes, the Chipola Cutoff runs three miles through Wewahitchka to the Apalachicola River, but the official river flows 14 miles further to its natural confluence with the Apalachicola. The Chipola contributes about 11 percent of the wide Apalachicola's flow, the largest single contributor in the state. At the river's confluence with the Apalachicola, it is another 26 miles to Apalachicola Bay.

Morning scene along the upper Chipola River.

Above: The Ovens cave off the Chipola River below the Florida Caverns State Park is the only known consistently dry cave along a Florida river. Only at flood stage will it be inundated.
Below: Chipola rock garden at the entrance of the Ovens.

Sunrise along the Merritt's Mill Pond, where several springs feed into the Chipola River.

Paddleboarder on the Dead Lakes section of the Chipola River.

The Chipola boasts 63 springs, more than any other Northwest Florida river, and it is known for its unique shoal bass. The water is generally clear at moderate to low water levels. At higher water levels, the water can be muddied by runoff. A trip down the Chipola is a memorable journey through rural north Florida with each segment offering unique experiences.

WAKULLA

The Wakulla River powers forth from a massive spring in Wakulla Springs State Park. At 185 feet deep and a football field wide, it is one of the largest in the world. The river that it spawns is as scenic as any in the state,

and visitors can take guided jungle boats through the upper mile-and-a-half to gawk at alligators, manatees, and an array of wading birds. The two-mile stretch below where these tour boats turn around is perhaps the wildest stretch of river anywhere in the state. Known as the sanctuary, only people doing periodic wildlife counts in canoes are allowed to enter. Here, the numbers of birds and alligators are higher than at any other part of the river as signs of humans are absent—no trash, no motorcraft, only a wild river and its creatures.

Below the first bridge along the Wakulla, where the state park boundary ends, the river is open to all sorts of watercraft. And like many spring-run rivers in summer, the Wakulla can be a busy place, especially on

Eternal youth was not to be found in the crystal depths of Florida's springs, but their mysterious caverns provided a source of much lore among the now-extinct Indian tribes. From them came water gods and many legends. One legend was that on moonlight nights hundreds of little people only four inches in height came and danced around the deeply submerged inflow of Wakulla Springs until a huge Indian warrior in a stone canoe appeared to drive them away—an illusion perhaps created by waving water plants and the moving shadow from a projecting rock in the springs. Scores of these legends, collected in book form, give a romantic overtone to the wonders viewed by tourists through glass-bottomed boats.

—WORKS PROGRESS ADMINISTRATION, *FLORIDA: A GUIDE TO THE SOUTHERNMOST STATE*, 1939

Wakulla River sunset.

The beach along Wakulla Springs in the state park is a popular warm-weather retreat.

weekends. So, it's great to paddle or go boating on the river on weekdays or early on weekend mornings to beat the crowds. Another advantage of early morning is that a cool mist often hovers above the water, and when the day starts to warm, it's wonderful to dip arms into the clear spring-fed water, and splash faces and head. Or, just jump in!

Osprey and red-shouldered hawks often call from the cypress canopy, and summer is a good time to spot the unmistakable silhouettes of swallow-tailed kites and Mississippi kites in the skies overhead. Numerous wading birds, anhinga, and cormorants can be seen along the shore in addition to sunning turtles and small- to medium-sized alligators. Occasionally, otters can be spotted—always a welcome sight—and seeing manatees is almost guaranteed.

A highlight one summer was taking off a couple of days from my day job and helping my friend Georgia with a youth kayak camp. I helped with a middle school group on a Wakulla paddling trip, and it was inspiring to see about a dozen young people take such an interest in the river's wildlife and beauty. Of course, we had our share of water fights, too!

One of the frontiers of paddle sports and wilderness pursuits in general is to get more young people outside, to pry them away from computers and other electronic gadgets, and the kayak camps and similar summer programs are a good start. Another frontier is to encourage more minority participation in outdoor pursuits, and it is heartening to see families of color paddling on the Wakulla. One reason is that the river is accessible, being 20 miles south of Tallahassee, and it is generally

Above: Affectionate manatees at Wakulla Springs.
Below: A baby alligator on its mother's back.

Above: Osprey hitting the surface of the Wakulla River.
Below: Preening egret in spring plumage.

safe because wildlife officers are often patrolling. It's also easy to rent a kayak or canoe. An outfitter is right on the water at Highway 98 (the "lower bridge"). Paddling from upper bridge to lower bridge is only about four miles and it's a good trip for beginners, or you can paddle upstream from Highway 98 and then back down.

For a coastal feel, travel downstream about three miles from Highway 98 to the launch at Fort San Marcos de Apalache in St. Marks, or at the St. Marks City Park on river left. The city park launch, however, is difficult to access at low tide. There are a couple of seafood restaurants in St. Marks that make for good end-of-trip destinations. You can bike down to St. Marks, too, on the Tallahassee-St. Marks Historic Railroad State Trail.

Full moons on the river can be magical, and of course the Wakulla is wonderful during the cooler months too, with more ducks and manatees to see and fewer crowds.

Right: A juvenile yellow-crowned night heron along the Wakulla River.
Below: A sunset/full moon kayak group on the lower Wakulla River.

Upper St. Marks River above Natural Bridge, with the trees in bright green spring foliage.

ST. MARKS

The St. Marks River can be divided into three parts: upper, middle and lower. The first two sections are separated by a half-mile span of land known as Natural Bridge, where the river ducks underwater in a series of sinkholes and emerges again in a wide stretch of river known as "the Basin."

Above Natural Bridge, the river is wild and mostly state-owned. It is a paddler's paradise if only the main channel would stay clear, but snags are commonplace. If you're willing to negotiate a few obstacles, you can launch at Natural Bridge and make your way upstream about three miles to Horn Springs, a large second-magnitude spring that is one of the more remote in the state. Chances are you won't see another human. Some massive old-growth cypress, most of them hollow, invite inspection. Above Horn Springs, the river is even more remote and snag-ridden, so allow lots of extra time if attempting it.

Natural Bridge is worth exploring as several springs and sinkholes dot the area. The Battle of Natural Bridge, reenacted every March, occurred in 1865 as Union troops advanced along the eastern shore of the river with hopes of capturing Tallahassee. Attempting to cross the natural land bridge, the troops were met with hostile resistance from mostly elderly men and young cadets and eventually were forced to retreat. Tallahassee stood proudly as the only southern capital not captured during the war.

Unless you know a private landowner, the only way to access "the Basin," a wide marshy area where the St. Marks River rises from underground below Natural Bridge, is to launch at the Newport Bridge along U.S. 98 and paddle upstream six miles and back down again. It's worth the trip if you're a good paddler and want a workout. A small motorboat would work, too, unless the river is at low water levels.

The St. Marks Basin is generally filled with birds. In winter, hundreds of white-beaked American coots usually frequent the marshes along with smaller flocks of wood ducks and other waterfowl. There are also wading birds galore—mostly great and snowy egrets, white ibis, and little and great blue herons. A bald eagle often makes a regal appearance along with more raucous red-shouldered hawks.

Below the Basin, where the river narrows and has a defined channel, houses dot the west bank for about a mile, but after this, the river shorelines are undeveloped. The water is often clear, especially in winter, and polarized glasses enable paddlers to peer into the depths to spot gar, sheepshead, bass, schools of mullet, and huge carp. Occasionally, an otter will peer above the surface at the curious humans, and in warmer months, a manatee or two are commonly seen just before the bridge.

A shallow area about halfway to the bridge can at times show a touch of whitewater and be deemed a class-one-half rapids. I rescued one paddler who tipped in the river near this spot, but it wasn't due to these mild rapids. A beginning paddler, she simply missed a tight turn and banked against a protruding log. When she popped up from the cold water, the first thing she announced was "I'm . . . afraid . . . of . . . snakes!"

"Don't worry," I assured her. "Most snakes are sunning themselves in the branches this time of day and they're not going to come after you." I guided her and her kayak to shore. As we emptied water from the boat, I carefully shielded from view a five-foot brown water snake wrapped around a branch behind me. Once I relaunched her, I said, pointing, "Just so you know, there is a very harmless brown water snake in that branch there that didn't even stir when we came ashore." She let out a scream, and I immediately regretted saying anything about it.

The middle St. Marks River is generally fine for beginners, but accidents can still happen.

Like most rivers, the St. Marks is rich in history. Native Americans once lived along its shores in much larger numbers than people do today. The river was a lifeblood for food, water, and a canoe path to numerous places.

In the early 1800s, after most Native Americans were driven from the area, white settlements were built along the shores, but some were short-lived. The most notable of these was Port Leon below the town of St. Marks. Once consisting of eight or ten businesses, a hotel, tavern, and warehouses, an 1843 hurricane and massive storm surge—some described it as a tidal wave—destroyed the town only a few years after it was founded.

Magnolia was a small but busy port town founded in 1827 above Newport. Cotton was often shipped for Jefferson County planters, and by 1830 the town became the second largest in middle Florida with a population of 276. But when a new mule-drawn railroad from Tallahassee to St. Marks bypassed the town in 1837, Magnolia was slowly abandoned and the 1843 hurricane wiped out most of what was left. All that remains of Magnolia today is a wooded cemetery.

Below Newport, the St. Marks widens and takes on a more coastal appearance as it flows past the port

1842 drawing of the extinct town of Magnolia on the St. Marks River. FLORIDA MEMORY

Sunset at the Fort San Marcos de Apalache Historic State Park.

town of St. Marks. At the historic Fort San Marcos de Apalache Historic State Park, where Native Americans, Spanish settlers, pirates, and American colonists vied for control of this strategic point for almost 300 years, the St. Marks joins with the Wakulla River and winds another five miles to the open Gulf of Mexico. This stretch makes for a nice paddling trip with several tree islands and side creeks to explore. Motorboat traffic can be heavy on weekends and holidays, however.

So, whether you're looking for history or wildlife, or both, try exploring the St. Marks River.

WACISSA

Great blue herons stand sentinel-like. An eagle peeps from a tall cypress while a trilling kingfisher zooms past. Otters and turtles poke their heads up, while an occasional alligator or water snake slides off the shore.

As the sun dips low, owl calls echo across the marshy vista and wading birds begin to roost.

The spring-fed Wacissa River is known for its wildlife, and it rarely disappoints. The upper river is wide and marshy, perfect for wading birds and alligators. Nearly 20 springs form the 15-mile river, all occurring in the upper mile and a half. The largest is known as Big Blue, about 45 feet deep and 60 feet wide. It's a favorite swimming hole for people in summer, and a large alligator sometimes stands guard atop a swimming raft in winter.

Most people explore the upper stretch of the river and return to the launch at a county-run park near the headsprings. A few run the river from the headsprings to a spot known as Goose Pasture, about 10 miles. The course of the river narrows and widens at various points, sometimes appearing open and marshy; at other times, shoreline trees form a tight canopy.

A spring evening on the upper Wacissa River.

A great blue heron walking a tree limb.

Above: Brown water snakes mating along the river.
Below: A dragonfly pauses on a blade of wild rice along the Wacissa River.

A preening limpkin.

The purple gallinule is one of the most striking birds one will see along a Florida river.

Below Goose Pasture, a few hardy souls venture down what is known as the Slave Canal. Built in the 1850s by enslaved African Americans to connect the Wacissa and Lower Aucilla rivers, the waterway is famous for its wild beauty—and for its challenges. In low water, numerous limestone rocks and logs inhibit passage. In high water, several side channels along the lower Wacissa divert the flow before the canal and can invite unwary paddlers to take a wrong fork. The result is a tangle of downed trees and branches and even more

Purple flag iris along the Wacissa.

choices for side channels. The rugged maze only gets worse. If the paddler keeps taking the right fork, that will usually lead to the braid that is free of snags.

This lower stretch of the river and Slave Canal boasts centuries-old cypresses and other large hardwoods such as swamp maple and bay. A tangle of climbing vines had given some trees the appearance of a green leafy cascade. "We say about the Slave Canal that we go in and come out, as if it had a door hinged at either end, curtained with vines—Virginia creeper and wild grape. A passage. Rite of passage," wrote author Janisse Ray in the 2004 *Between Two Rivers* (Cerulean et al., eds.) anthology.

Water is usually cool and clear, or tinted yellow or light brown or golden, depending on sunlight. Mullet dart away like miniature torpedoes, and small and large alligators are often seen. This is as wild as anything Florida has to offer, a true bush paddler's paradise. As an old saying suggests, it's not the destination but the getting there that counts.

In late spring, the area's wildness causes some paddlers to avoid it. April and May is the alligator mating season, and yellow flies can be pesky.

Most of the river corridor was purchased by the state of Florida in 2000 and 2003 and added to the 50,471-acre Aucilla Wildlife Management Area. The Wacissa River, including the Slave Canal, was designated a Florida canoe trail by the governor and cabinet in 1970. It is now one of about 70 designated Florida paddling trails.

Bright-red cardinal flowers and purple-flowered pickerelweed line parts of the comparatively wide waterway—more than 50 feet across in some places—along with white blossoms of duck potato and swamp lily. Tiger swallowtail butterflies add movement and more color.

In past years, several paddlers have spent the night looking for the Slave Canal. Before a sign was posted, many overshot the entrance and ended up in the Aucilla River, paddling until they literally ran out of river. The river swirls underground in a huge sinkhole. It's commonplace for the Aucilla. From its origin near Boston, Georgia, the Aucilla plays a disappearing act several times before rising for the last time at Nutall Rise, just above Highway 98 and less than six miles from the Gulf, not far from the terminus of the Slave Canal.

Friends of my parents missed the Slave Canal entrance several years ago. By the time they realized their error and ended up in Half-Mile Rise, part of the disappearing Aucilla, the sun was dipping low and it was too late to paddle upstream back to their launch spot at Goose Pasture. They quickly learned that a canoe makes for a poor bed. The Wacissa doesn't reveal its passages easily, especially in summertime, and conditions change from season to season and year to year.

Kayakers pause by the Wacissa Slave Canal.

Boulders along the Slave Canal are evidence of enslaved people enlarging the waterway in the 1850s to create a shipping canal.

Once on the canal, the lush swampy wilderness and occasional sightings of wading birds, brightly colored warblers, alligators, wild turkey, and deer make for an enjoyable trip. You almost forget that this lush waterway was built by human hands with shovels and pickaxes until you spot stacks of moss-covered limestone rocks and boulders lining the canal. It is an eerie reminder in this more "enlightened" age. Enslaved people were forced to labor in wet humid conditions, fighting bugs and malaria, and contending with all sorts of misery and discomfort. Nature has almost erased signs of that toil. Almost.

The canal was an attempt to open a shipping channel for cotton, tobacco, and other goods, built during a period of canal fever spawned by completion of the Erie Canal in 1825. But alas, the Slave Canal's full potential was never realized. It wasn't deep enough, and railroads were soon established in the region. Today, mostly nature-loving paddlers enjoy the fruits of that early labor, along with Gulf-spawned striped mullet. Mullet schools are everywhere.

At one point, the FWC, as part of a statewide effort toward racial sensitivity in regard to geographic names, proposed renaming the waterway "Cotton Run Canal." The Jefferson County Commission and several individuals familiar with the canal, including African American leaders, opposed the name change. In January 2006, the U.S. Board on Geographic Names agreed with the opponents, citing a lack of local support for the change. The Slave Canal remains the official name, serving to remind visitors of the men who toiled on this sometimes paradisiacal waterway.

Perhaps appropriately, the Slave Canal is not an easy waterway to navigate. The entire trip from Goose Pasture on the lower Wacissa to Nutall Rise on the Aucilla near Highway 98 is only five miles, but it can take four to five hours, sometimes longer. If the water level is low, you'll scrape limestone rocks and shoals in several places. Snags are numerous at any water level, and it takes skill and coordination to pull boats over huge logs without slipping and getting wet. The most challenging part can be near the bottom where tidal influence is evident. At low tide, rocks are covered with dark mud, and a long shoals area is too shallow to paddle. Paddlers must carefully pull their boats through the uninviting slippery goo. Snags are easy compared to that mess.

I've also been on the canal when it's overcast and raining. Without the sun, the swamp forest and water appear darker and more foreboding. I don't want to leave the security of my kayak, but then I have to stop and pull over a snag, stepping into unknown depths.

It's more difficult to suppress primal fears of creepy crawly things—sharp-toothed alligators, snakes, spiders. Did I mention the many spiders? And then there are the echoes of those poor souls who dug the canal. I imagine them lingering there in the dislodged boulders. Perhaps a part of them, their sacrifice, has never left the canal.

Amid the shadows, however, I often spot white-tailed deer. It's difficult to be gloomy around spry deer. That also goes for the leaping mullet making their way up the narrow channel from the Gulf of Mexico like southern salmon. No one knows for sure why they jump. Perhaps it's for the sheer joy of living! Smells come out more in the rain, too, especially sweet aromas of willow, red bay, and brilliant white swamp lilies.

After a Slave Canal rainstorm has passed, sunlight envelops the swamp and highlights a dazzling array of color. Leaves, flowers, mosses—all seem to leap out in glistening brilliance. It is then I realize why I came, and why I will return again and again.

ICHETUCKNEE

The Ichetucknee boasts at least nine springs, which help to keep the water temperature a cool 72 degrees. The world-famous Ichetucknee is a river of dual personalities. In summer, the river is swamped with folks cooling off by floating down the river in a colorful array of inner tubes and rafts. In cooler weather, kayakers and canoeists—in far fewer numbers—paddle the river, enjoying a quiet wild beauty within Ichetucknee Springs State Park. No motorboats are allowed in the park.

The Florida Park Service carefully regulates the number of summer visitors so that the river, especially the more fragile upper stretch, can recover during the rest of the year. Year-round, the river supports an array of wildlife and fish that includes otters, Suwannee bass, and the loggerhead musk turtle. The river boasts an impressive 44 species of fish along with 11 aquatic turtle species, making it one of the most diverse turtle rivers in North America. In addition, the Ichetucknee silt snail found in Coffee Spring lives nowhere else in the world, one reason why some of the springs are closed off to paddlers and tubers.

Before state park protection in 1970, the Ichetucknee was a river abused. Shorelines and springs were severely eroded by human use. Litter, mostly beer cans and bottles, numbered in the thousands. I was an eyewitness, having canoed the river in 1969 with my boy scout troop. We tried to clean up as best we could, but the task was nearly insurmountable and we had no way of disposing of the mountains of refuse. What we did find in camping along the shore was a fat rattlesnake more than six feet in length. Our scoutmaster deemed it a threat, and what ensued was a pitched

Kayakers pause while paddling the Ichetucknee River.

The Ichetucknee and its run, the most beautiful landscape in the world.

—ARCHIE CARR, *A NATURALIST IN FLORIDA*

battle between adolescents throwing rocks and a strik-ing snake. The rattler lost, and to this day I regret the incident as rattlesnakes are generally nonaggressive and this one likely wouldn't have bothered us.

Once the Florida Park Service took over manage-ment, it took on tasks of revegetating shorelines and spring edges, cleaning up the trash, and regulating uses. No disposable containers of any kind are allowed on the water, so litter and broken glass are almost nonexistent. Plus, the side springs are closed to watercraft, although a couple are accessible by land trail and open for swim-ming. If snorkeling the deep headwater springs, gazing into azure depths through a mask, you can ponder the words of writer Al Burt: "The Ichetucknee's waters bubble up out of the ground and flow like melted dia-monds across a sandy bottom through a natural forest."

The Ichetucknee's rich history includes an early 1600s Spanish mission near its banks, Santa Catalina de Afucia. The mission was destroyed by raiding Yamasee Indians in 1685, and many of the Timucua Indians associated with the mission were either killed or enslaved.

In the 1700s, Seminole Indians established a village near where the Ichetucknee meets the Santa Fe River. The village was known as Ichetucknee, which means "pond of the beaver."

During the Second Seminole War, the Ichetucknee was mentioned in a passage by army surgeon J. R. Motte in *Journey into Wilderness* (1837): "About noon of the second day's march from Charles' ferry we reached an oasis in this desert, which broke upon our vision like the fairy-land sometimes seen in dreams. Itchetuckney [*sic*] was the name of this terrestrial paradise, for such it seemed to our weary faculties."

Today, the Ichetucknee River is viewed as a paradise by almost 200,000 visitors a year, the majority coming in summer.

SANTA FE

The 75-mile Santa Fe River originates in Lake Santa Fe near Keystone Heights and flows north of Gainesville before doing what several other Florida rivers do—swirl underground. The phenomenon was accurately described by J. R. Motte in 1837:

The Santa Fe River in O'Leno State Park just before it swirls underground for three miles.

Whiskey Springs is one of several large springs feeding the Santa Fe River.

About eight miles from Newnansville we crossed the Santa-Fee [Santa Fe] river, over the natural bridge. Had we not been told by our guide at the moment, we should never have suspected that there was anything like a river in our vicinity. This spot exhibited another specimen of Nature's freaks, which I have already noticed; but here it was on a much larger scale. The river, which a week previous had overflowed this spot to a swimming depth, and a width of half a mile, now passed quietly underground a distance of three miles, forming a natural bridge of that width; when it again emerges into daylight, and shows itself flowing in a broad and deep channel.

The natural bridge had been used as a Native American trail for millennia because it bypassed the need for a river crossing. The Spanish followed it as well and used it as part of their east-west mission trail, also known as El Camino Real, the Royal Road. It ran from the Apalachee Province near present-day Tallahassee to St. Augustine. The Bellamy Road, built in the early 1800s by the American government, generally followed the same route. The spot where the Santa Fe River disappears underground is now part of O'Leno State Park, one of the first state parks built by the Civilian Conservation Corps in the 1930s. The river reemerges three miles later at River Rise State Park and flows another 35 miles to the Suwannee River. Most of the large springs for which the river is renowned are between High Springs and the Suwannee. These include Gilchrist Blue, now a state park, Rum Island, Ginnie, and Lily.

Lily Springs is smaller than most of its counterparts but was best known for its longtime caretaker, Naked

A sign warning paddlers that Naked Ed is ahead at Lily Springs along the Santa Fe River.

Ed, one of the last of Florida's colorful hermits. For many years he lived in a tiny hut near the spring and generally wore a loincloth or his birthday suit, weather permitting. Since 1986, Ed Watts, alias Naked Ed, took care of Lily Springs and greeted paddlers. On one mid-winter visit, we found the bearded naturist fully clothed and sitting beside a fire in front of his palm frond–covered hut. The only thing naked was his prominent bald head. Temperatures in the 50s evidently deterred the famous hermit, but he did say he stripped down on a recent cold day at the request of visitors from Michigan who knew of his fame. "I hate to disappoint people," he said. "I've posed for pictures with all kinds of people, even church groups. And a few will actually take their clothes off, too, for a dip in the springs. But if they're uncomfortable with me being naked, I'll slip on a loincloth, especially if kids are around." I had heard that Ed had a collection of different loincloths, but he didn't volunteer to show them to us.

Ed was surprised to see anyone paddling the river given the earlier rain and cool weather, and he regaled us with stories of how he prevented people from trashing the springs and turning it into a party spot and how he was interviewed every semester by University of Florida journalism students—usually pretty young women, he said. But what was really on his mind was the potential sale of the 10-acre Lily property since it had been up for sale. He was helping the owners screen would-be buyers. "You can tell if they're serious or not," he said. Of course, Ed wanted to continue being the caretaker of Lily Springs if it was sold. "I'd hate to leave this place," he said.

Numerous hand-lettered signs posted on trees reminded guests of Ed's philosophy of nonjudgment regarding nudity—"I'm not qualified to cast the first stone. Are you?" Other signs advocated a respect for nature, and one asserted that "man is the most dangerous animal in the jungle."

Ed said he loved having respectful and sober visitors, especially "girls in their 20s," although he assured them he was harmless. What would a Santa Fe River Adam fantasize about other than an Eve? People often wondered if Ed was simply a lecherous old man or some kind of folk hero. Perhaps he was an amalgamation of both.

Ed's public nudity emerged from a childhood disease. He was born with brittle bone disease and he spent a lot of time in hospitals, becoming accustomed

River otters are always fun to watch on a river trip.

to being naked in front of nurses and doctors. Once he was an adult, after working various jobs, it became dangerous for him to work since he could so easily break bones. He once broke a rib while coughing. He began to receive government disability and wanted to move to a place where he would be comfortable in his birthday suit and people would be comfortable with—or tolerate—him. A 1985 canoe trip down the Santa Fe River turned him on to Lily Springs, and the dire need to clean it up, and so a rent-free arrangement was made with the owners. Ed became the unofficial care-taker. And so the renowned "wild man of Lily Springs" was born. Ailments forced Ed to leave his beloved Lily a few years after our visit, but the legend lives on. A beer in High Springs still bears his name—Naked Ed's Pale Ale.

St. Petersburg Times reporter Jeff Klinkenberg penned an article about Naked Ed in 2005. "Ed is a throwback to an era mostly gone," Klinkenberg concluded. "Once every corner of our state boasted a genuine eccentric living in the woods or on the water. But like panthers and crocodiles, few were able to survive civilized Florida. Yet Real Florida hangs on. There are woods and swamps just big enough to harbor endangered wildlife,

and a few hidey holes that can shelter an endangered hermit or two."

Another Florida river once harbored a well-known hermit. The "wild man of the Loxahatchee"—Trapper Nelson—was a Tarzan-like figure in Southeast Florida from the 1930s until the mid-1960s. Often going shirtless (not naked) to reveal his muscular physique and barrel chest, Nelson would entertain visitors with a huge indigo snake draped over his shoulders. He trapped animals for fur and operated a small zoo along the river. His homestead is now part of Jonathan Dickinson State Park (see the Loxahatchee River discussion).

On almost every trip down the Santa Fe River, what is apparent is that the river environs serve as a wildlife haven. Myriad plate-sized turtles usually poke their heads above the surface or sun on logs. Numerous birds line the shores or dart across the waterway—great egrets, wood ducks, wood storks, white ibis, anhingas, bald eagles, great blue herons, crows, red-shouldered hawks, pileated woodpeckers, and kingfishers. Most are in pairs and seem unafraid. "It's like Noah's Ark," one friend observed. Indeed, if Noah had needed a near-complete representation of North Florida riverine

A tricolored heron hunts for a meal with great patience.

wildlife species, he would have come to the Santa Fe River. But would there have been any room for hermits in his survivalist scheme?

Among the highlights of any Florida trip are river otters frolicking along the shore. On one Santa Fe River trip, a pair of otters dove into the water as we approached and ducked into a den inside an embankment. We could hear them inside, communicating in a language only known to otters, their voices echoing in what was likely a small cave.

As much as the Santa Fe is a wildlife haven, it does have its share of problematic issues and threats. Over the past few years, the river has had chronically low water levels, a result of below-average rainfall combined with increased aquifer withdrawals. And still, water bottlers seek to withdraw more water from the river's springs. Opposition has been growing and some proposals have been defeated or delayed, especially in light of periodic historically low water levels. The low water was evident at one rocky stretch where we had

to step out of our watercraft and push them along the shallow stretch for 30 feet. And only a quarter-mile above the Highway 27 Bridge, a rocky span 50 feet wide completely blocked the river.

The Santa Fe's water quality has become degraded over the past few years, too. Massive algae blooms are sometimes apparent, especially near blockages where there is inadequate flushing. Litter is another issue, mostly during the warm months below the launch for tubers at the privately owned Ginnie Springs. Despite frequent cleanups, the number of bottles and cans (mostly beer) below the tube launch can be problematic. Perhaps the river needs more caretakers like Naked Ed.

HOMOSASSA

The Homosassa River has long been enjoyed by visitors to Florida as evidenced by this 1908 account by A. W. Dimock, writing in *Florida Enchantments*:

A manatee peers into the Fish Bowl at Homosassa Springs State Park.

Large snook seen through the Fish Bowl window.

On our second day we were rowed slowly up the river, viewing with much interest the oak, red cedar, palmetto and great flowering magnolia on its banks. Countless thousands of ducks were dotting the water on every side and in the broad shallows mullet leaped high in the air, hundreds in every minute. At the head of the river we floated on the famous Homosassa Spring out of which boils the river. The spring is almost circular, about a hundred feet in diameter and sixty in depth, and through its crystal clearness the smallest fish can be distinctly seen. As we lunched upon its bank a wild turkey lit upon a tree above us, mockingbirds sang to us and a cardinal bird inquired if we intended to leave any crumbs. As I gazed on the marvelous spring, in the perfect peace of that balmy day, the spirit of the Fountain possessed me and I dreamed that I had found what Ponce de Leon so long and so vainly sought. Now, after many years which have taken their lawful toll of the body, I can yet believe that Perpetual Youth of the spirit is one of the Florida Enchantments.

For the paddler, the Homosassa River can best be enjoyed during the week as the river can be busy on weekends and holidays. This tropical-looking stream is rich in wading birds and manatees. The spring itself is part of Homosassa Springs State Park and therefore cannot be accessed from the water, but the park is worth a land visit because you can descend into the spring via a giant "Fish Bowl" that has windows in every direction. From inside this underwater observatory an amazing variety of both fresh- and saltwater fish can be spotted, from snook to tarpon to bluegill. Manatee also frequent the spring, especially on cold winter days, and it's fun to look squarely into the face of the humble sea cow from inside the Fish Bowl. The park also features an array of mostly native animals and birds such as panther, deer, black bear, and bald eagle.

The most famous inhabitant of Homosassa Springs State Park is not a native Florida animal but a hippopotamus named Lucifer, "Lu" for short. Lu is the lone holdover from when the park housed celebrity animals in the 1960s, stars of television shows like *Gentle Ben*, *Flipper*, and *Daktari*. Soon after the Florida Park Service took control of Homosassa in 1989, a proposal was put forth to remove Lu. School children protested and started a letter-writing campaign, prompting then Governor Lawton Chiles to declare Lu an honorary Florida citizen and therefore qualified for permanent housing at the park. As of 2021, Lu was still going strong at Homosassa, entertaining visitors by opening its huge jaws while a volunteer tossed in cantaloupes, squash, and other vegetarian fare, vying to become the oldest hippo in captivity.

The name "Homosassa" dates back to early Native American inhabitants. It means "a place where wild pepper grows" in the Seminole-Creek language.

CHAZ

The name "Chassahowitzka" near Homosassa Springs is a mouthful. It is believed to mean either "hanging pumpkin" or "river of lazy waters" in the Muscogee language—so locals just call it the Chaz.

According to outdoor writer Rube Allyn in his 1957 book, *Outdoors Afloat*, the river environs were once occupied by Seminole Indians and runaway slaves until they were routed by "renegade whites" who squatted on the land since before the Civil War. Regarding one spring, Allyn wrote, "This spot is a deep spring in the river where the skeletons of warriors who lost their lives defending it, still repose." A skull and crossbones sign marked the spring, he said, a sign that has long since disappeared.

The Chaz can be a busy place these days, and its springs are afflicted by high nitrates like many Florida springs, but the clear pools are nonetheless alluring with their variation. You can paddle or motor to several of them from the county launch.

Located in the river's upper reaches, some of the springs are easy to reach and others are not, but all are worth the effort. From the launch, be sure to go upstream just 150 feet to Chassahowitzka Springs and just a few more minutes to Seven Sisters Spring, a deep circular pool. Spend some time enjoying this gem, and bring a mask and snorkel. As you move downstream, don't ignore the small tributaries. One leads to Crab Creek Spring where there is a single home and a lush lagoon.

Docked boats along the upper Chassahowitzka River.

Sunset on the lower Chassahowitzka.

Baird Creek, only a half-mile below the launch, is narrow and canopied, leading to Blue Spring. There are more than 30 blue springs in Florida, but none disappoint, and neither does Blue Spring along the Chaz. You can follow Baird Creek further, and if it becomes too shallow to paddle, do some shallow wading to the Crack. This spring emanates from a rocky crevice.

Below the spring area, the Chaz widens and becomes more coastal in appearance as it continues through the Chassahowitzka National Wildlife Refuge along marsh and low-lying hardwood hammocks. A few private tree islands include rustic Old Florida fishing shacks. Wildlife throughout the river system can be abundant with bald eagles, wood ducks, manatees, otters, alligators, and wading birds. Total distance to the Gulf is only six miles, but the many springs make a trip on the Chaz a full day-trip.

WEEKI WACHEE

In 1946, Walton Hall Smith and Newt Perry built an underwater theater in a breathtaking setting—a massive gin-clear spring with exposed limestone rock and a steep drop to a vent 185 feet deep, one of 33 Florida springs considered first magnitude. Promoters labeled it the "Mountain Underwater." But the spring already had an exotic name—Weeki Wachee. And when the attraction opened to the public on October 12, 1947, with local teens playing the mermaid roles but without the tails, Weeki Wachee became the only spring in the world that featured live mermaids.

Weeki Wachee Spring also spawns a river by the same name, eight miles long and clear until it nears the Gulf, with eelgrass swaying in the current and wading birds lining the shores. Silvery mullet frequently leap skyward, glinting in sunlight, while manatees often make their way upstream from the Gulf on cold winter days.

The river brims with people on warm weekends with numerous canoes and kayaks heading downstream and motorized vessels making their way upstream from the Gulf. The state park also operates a busy water park near the headsprings. The mermaid shows continue to be popular, and mermaids no longer have to wave at drivers along U.S. Highway 19 to lure in customers.

Weeki Wachee reached its peak during the mid-1960s. Then along came Interstate Highway 75. It began to siphon travelers from U.S. 19. Weeki Wachee suffered. The attraction changed hands several times until the state of Florida took ownership. Florida's 160th state park opened in 2008. Former mermaids, whose motto is "Once a mermaid, always a mermaid," are still actively involved with the attraction, and the Mermaids of Yesteryear shows are often sold out. Current and former mermaids describe working at the attraction as a "sisterhood" where everyone knows each other's business and lifelong friendships are made.

A mermaid performer once said that to dive into the strong current of the spring was like trying to swim up a waterfall. It took fortitude and athleticism, and the performers had to smile and make it look effortless while performing an elaborate underwater ballet. Not surprisingly, today's mermaids have to be scuba certified. About 30 mermaids are employed at the park, and several of these are often on the road, promoting Weeki Wachee at venues around the country.

We lined up on the bank. Our test was to swim across the spring and back without drowning, and if we made it, and we all did, we were all mermaids all of a sudden.

—MARY DARLINGTON
FLETCHER, IN *WEEKI
WACHEE: CITY OF
MERMAIDS* BY LU VICKERS
AND SARA DIONNE,
REMEMBERING THE FIRST
MERMAID TRYOUTS

A kayaker on the clear-flowing Weeki Wachee River.

Rainbow Springs State Park features several natural-looking waterfalls.

RAINBOW

The upper Rainbow River is a sparkling kaleidoscope of emerald-green eelgrass. Wood ducks, anhinga, heron, and ibis are often perched in branches, and river otters—with their insulated fur—are often seen swimming the river. As a result, the Rainbow River is a draw for multitudes of tubers and paddlers during the warm months, and Rainbow Springs is popular with swimmers with its refreshing 72-degree temperatures.

Once a local hangout where phosphate was mined nearby, Rainbow Springs began a transformation to popular roadside attraction in 1937 when Frank Greene and F. E. Hemphill bought the property. They changed the name from Blue Springs to Rainbow Springs and the spring run from Blue Run to the Rainbow River. It was a brilliant public relations strategy. While there are several Blue Springs in state of Florida, Rainbow Springs was a new moniker that conjured up a multi-faceted jewel of color.

A handsome lodge and tourist cabins were built, and a simulated paddle-wheel boat known as the Rainbow Queen carried passengers downriver. To view the spring's wonders from a unique vantage point, half-submerged "submarine boats" enabled visitors to sit below the water line, much like the submerged giant Fish Bowl at Homosassa Springs—only these fish bowls were able to move. The hilly shoreline was conducive to the creation of waterfalls, the largest one known as Rainbow Falls—"the only scenic waterfall in Florida"—built from mining rubble.

Attendance at Rainbow Springs steadily rose and hit a plateau in 1965, just before the new Interstate 75 began carrying nearly three times more tourists than U.S. Highways 19, 27, 441, and 41 combined. Still, the attraction hung on for several more years as extra features were added to make the 18-mile drive from the interstate highway more worthwhile. The Leaf Ride monorail, featuring leaf-shaped gondolas, was launched in the late 1960s along with a magnificent fountain with a rainbow backdrop. Simulated log rafts on the river added a more rustic experience for visitors. Bathing beauties in the form of mermaids were added, too, along with a synchronized swimming group known as the Bahama Belles.

Ownership of Rainbow Springs changed several times, and despite the new ideas and features, the attraction closed in 1974—three years after Disney World opened—and the infrastructure fell into disrepair. Local citizens eventually put together a coalition to seek public ownership, and the state of Florida purchased Rainbow Springs in 1990. It opened as a state park in 1995 with great fanfare. Like many "Golden

Left: Most Florida rivers feature the anhinga, commonly called the snake bird due to its long neck and the way it swims underwater. This is a female.
Above: The anhinga must skewer their fish and then eat them headfirst so that the spines don't cut their esophagus.

Like most spring-fed streams, the Rainbow River is a good place to spot wildlife, such as immature bald eagles.

Age of Tourism" attractions that were adopted by the state, increased emphasis was placed on conservation and nature-based recreation. Rainbow Falls and several other side falls, by this time beautifully lined with ferns and moss-covered boulders as if they had always been there, remained as park attractions while the submarine boats and Leaf Ride monorail were not salvageable. No longer a huge tourist attraction, swimming, paddling, boating, and tubing continue to draw crowds to Rainbow Springs and Rainbow River, especially in summer.

SILVER

Florida has 33 first-magnitude springs, and Silver Springs is the largest and most famous, the three main headwater springs pumping out more than 550 million gallons a day. Tourists have long flocked to the group of azure springs, first by steamboat and then by stagecoach, train, and automobile. And though impacted by high nitrogen and algae like most of Florida's springs, Silver Springs is still a vision of beauty. The average

clarity and blue tint are impressive, and the five-mile spring run boasts a total of 30 springs.

The springs have intriguing names such as Mastodon Bone Spring, Alligator Hole Spring, Garden of Eden Spring, No Name Cove Springs, Turtle Nook Spring, Turtle Meadows Spring, and Raccoon Island Spring. The largest is Mammoth Spring near the glass-bottom boat loading dock. The spring pool measures 300 by 200 feet across. All of the springs are accessible to paddlers and slow-speed boaters, although swimming is not allowed in any of them.

When cruising the scenic river, the shores almost entirely state-owned, one is struck by the wildlife—turtles, alligators, and an array of wading birds that seem almost oblivious to humans. There are troops of exotic rhesus macaque monkeys, too, descendants of ones placed on an island by a tour boat operator in the 1930s who mistakenly thought rhesus macaque monkeys couldn't swim. They swim fine, and they also reproduce just fine in their Florida home, much to the chagrin of wildlife biologists who fear a detrimental impact on native wildlife. They also carry the deadly

On a clear and calm day, after the sun has attained sufficient altitude, the view from one of the glass-bottom boats is beautiful and entrancing, almost beyond description. The impression left upon the mind of the visitor is wonderful, for every feature on the bottom of this gigantic basin is as clear and distinct as if the water had been removed and atmosphere substituted in its place. It is like looking down from some lofty perch upon a fairy scene of beauty and magic.

—NEVIN O. WINTER, *FLORIDA, THE LAND OF ENCHANTMENT*, 1918

Herpes B virus, so a wide berth is advised and no feeding is allowed.

The Silver River was most likely a series of sinkholes thousands of years ago when the water table was significantly lower, thus the reason mastodon and other prehistoric animal bones have been found inside the caves. Early Native Americans once hunted these creatures, and evidence of their presence was found as

well. It has been said that if human history in the area were measured on a 12-inch ruler, Native Americans would occupy 11.5 inches or more.

Today, since the main Silver Springs attraction was merged into the Florida State Park system in 2013, paddlers can launch near the headwaters for a small fee or rent boats from a park vendor. After five miles, you can take out at the county-run Ray's Wayside Park at

Silver River scene in winter.

Above: Rhesus macaque monkeys were introduced to the Silver River in the 1930s and continue to expand their population.
Below: Red-bellied slider turtles.

The Silver River is known for its wildlife, such as this black-crowned night heron.

the bottom of the spring run. Or, you can launch at Ray's and paddle upstream and then down. Motorboats can launch at Ray's as well and maintain a slow speed throughout the spring run.

Before cruising down the main river, the side channels in the upper section of the park are worth exploring. Here, you can see remnants of stops along a former jungle boat tour, including a Seminole village, log fort, and pioneer town.

ROCK SPRINGS RUN AND WEKIVA

Just a few miles above the many theme parks of Orlando lies a carefully protected subtropical wilderness where multiple springs feed the Rock Springs Run and Wekiva River system. If you embark in a canoe or kayak at King's Landing just below the "emerald cut," a clear sand-bottomed spring run for

Rock Springs, you will soon be enfolded by the curving trunks of sable palm and the arms of mature live oak trees festooned with resurrection fern. Swamp maple, sweetgum, dahoon holly, and sea myrtle shrubs add splashes of color, depending on the season, and the river channel is lined with dollarweed, waterweed, and pickerelweed. Eelgrass swirls in the gentle current. A few alligators and numerous turtles sun on logs while a wide assortment of wading birds poke in the water for their next meal.

The generally accepted interpretation for the name "Wekiva" and "Wekiwa," as both names are used, is that "Wekiva" means "flowing water" while "Wekiwa" means "spring of water." Most of the shoreline and much of the basin for the 24-mile river system is protected either by Rock Springs Run Preserve State Park, Wekiwa Springs State Park, the Lower Wekiva

Above: Paddleboarders on the Rock Springs Run just north of Orlando.
Below: Baby raccoon along Rock Springs Run.

Above: A blue-gray gnatcatcher.
Below: Rock Springs Run water moccasin.

Misty Wekiva spring-run at dawn.

Roseate spoonbill near Katie's Landing along the Wekiva River.

River Preserve State Park, and Seminole State Forest. The entire system is one of only two national wild and scenic rivers in the state. Four primitive campsites are set up for paddlers along Rock Springs Run and the Wekiva River. Camping along the river is a treat, and one is often serenaded at night by barred owls and chuck-will's-widows, a small songbird with a call much like a whippoorwill.

A mist-cloaked waterway often greets paddlers early in the morning. As sunlight begins to stream through the canopy, blue damselflies land on delicate grapevine tendrils while swallowtail butterflies flit about blooming duck potato, blue flag iris, and the white blossoms of titi. Sometimes mammals are spotted—raccoons, otters, and the occasional black bear. The surrounding wilderness is a well-known black bear refuge. Diversity in the river system is impressive: 120 species of birds, 8 species of turtles, and numerous threatened and endangered plants and animals. Scientists have labeled the area a global biodiversity hot spot.

Summers and weekends can be busy with people where the eight-mile Rock Springs Run merges with the spring run in Wekiwa Springs State Park. The park is easily accessible for more than a million people who live within 20 miles of its entrance, and it has been used as a retreat since the 1890s. Equally busy is a spot just below the spring run known as Wekiva Island, the location of a commercial outfitter, bar, and party spot perched along the water's edge. The family-owned establishment does boast rainwater-fed bathrooms and solar panels, but it can be a busy place with inexperienced paddlers zigzagging and bumping into trees, logs, and each other. This activity only lasts for a brief period, however, and peace and serenity can quickly return for the paddler, with abundant wildlife once again evident. A more hidden problem are nitrates that promote excessive weed growth in the river. Efforts are being made to reduce the thousands of septic tanks in the basin by hooking households to efficiently operated municipal sewage plants. Reducing fertilizer use on lawns, golf courses, and farms is also essential to nitrate control.

In all, Florida has protected more than 70,000 acres of the Wekiva River system. Few places in the country have rivers that emerge from a rapidly urbanizing area and almost immediately flow through vast tracts of wilderness. Decades of conservation land-buying programs in the state have yielded impressive results, depriving developers of choice properties.

Wekiva protection efforts began in earnest in 1982 with the establishment of the Friends of the Wekiva River. Six years later, the environmental group spearheaded passage of the Wekiva River Protection Act, which helped to safeguard wetlands, wildlife and habitat, and rural character within a 180-square mile protection area. This opened the way for the federal wild and scenic river designation in 2000. Despite the river's busy stretches, alligators, wading birds, and turtles easily outnumber people, even on busy weekends.

Numerous other springs and short spring runs are found in Florida, such as the popular Juniper Springs and Juniper Creek in the Ocala National Forest.

SWAMP STREAMS

Also called blackwater rivers, swamp streams are water bodies that drain cypress swamps and pine flatwoods and, as a result, their waters are normally stained from decomposing plant material. The color varies from black coffee or tea to red and yellow, depending on rainfall, depth, and the type of bottom material. For example, black water can appear red or yellow when flowing over a shallow sandbar, which is why author Betty Watts called these "red-black waters": "When visitors to Florida first look down on the historic Suwannee River, their reaction is likely to be surprise and disappointment. 'Why the water is *black. Tsch! Tsch!*'" she wrote in 1975. "Chemically, the pigments are akin to those in a cup of tea, and just as harmless."

Above: Glowing white against a blackwater river is a swamp lily blossom, commonly seen in later spring and summer along Florida rivers.
Left: The Sopchoppy River in Florida's Big Bend is a classic blackwater stream, emerging from swamps in the Apalachicola National Forest.

Above: The upper Perdido River along the Florida and Alabama border.
Below: Sunset and kayaks on Perdido Bay.

Blackwater Rivers are primarily found in the Amazon River basin and the southern United States, with Florida having a good share of these.

PERDIDO

The Perdido River hugs the Alabama and Florida border, flowing primarily through conservation lands in both states. Meaning "lost" in Spanish, the 63-mile river was in the center of an historic boundary dispute between England, Spain, France, and the United States. At one time, "West Florida," an English colony, even stretched to present-day Louisiana before eventually retreating to the current river boundary.

Due to its narrow and twisting nature and occasional snags, the upper Perdido is mostly suitable for canoes and kayaks, and Atlantic white cedar trees tower magnificently from the shores. The lower river is suitable for motorized crafts and is known for increasingly rare pitcher plant bogs. Both Alabama and Florida are beginning to feature this scenic stream. Alabama has put together six rustic river camp shelters for paddlers along the upper river, while the Nature Conservancy is erecting river camps along the lower river on the Florida side. These are all to encourage ecotourism and more multiday trips along this unspoiled waterway.

One advantage of fishing a waterway that runs along the border of two states is that a fishing license from either state will work. Just don't fish a tributary that is wholly within the state where you don't have a license.

BLACKWATER AND NEARBY STREAMS

When not in flood stage, Florida's rivers are often mellow streams where you can float and paddle and even close your eyes to swirl in the current with no worries, listening to birds and the river's song. The Florida Panhandle's Blackwater River is one such waterway, a highly popular river in summer and on warm weekends.

The gold-tinted Blackwater River in Blackwater River State Park.

Blooming mountain laurel along Juniper Creek, which feeds into the Blackwater River.

The Blackwater is perfect for floating and jumping out on the numerous brilliant white sandbars for which the river is known. Despite its name—Blackwater, or the original *Oka-lusa* (water black) in the Muscogee language—the water is often a transparent golden-brown. Most of the stream flows through undeveloped lands of the Blackwater State Forest and Blackwater River State Park, core areas of the largest contiguous longleaf pine/wiregrass ecosystem left in the world. "A forest like this is rarer than a tropical rainforest," said Callie DeHaven of the Nature Conservancy. The water seeping from this forest is as pure as it comes, merely tinted with tannins from leaves and roots of shoreline vegetation. No wonder the Blackwater River is so popular.

"I've been on all the rivers around here and this is still my favorite," said Paul Harville, a longtime employee at the Blackwater Canoe Rental. The business is open year-round, seven days a week, in all types of weather. The only time it closes is when the river is at flood stage, a rare occasion.

Tampa Bay Times reporter Terry Tomalin paddled the river for three days in single-digit, nearly record-breaking winter weather in 2012. Sane people slept in warm beds miles away. "Lying awake, waiting for morning, I wondered if spinal fluid can freeze," Tomalin wrote, "for it felt like every time I moved my backbone was about to snap. After hours of silent suffering, daylight came, but brought no relief. Everything was frozen, including camera and phone batteries, gas canisters and hatches to our kayaks, containing all our food and water, which was now turned to ice."

Those types of trips make for more interesting adventure stories, but what about the perfect days? It was sunny, beautiful, and the water was refreshing . . . snooze. Surely scary rednecks, snakes, alligators, tipping over, storms, bone-chilling cold, and such make for exciting stories. But the Blackwater is worthy of mention because it is one of those rivers where you can have a perfect trip when not too crowded—or too cold. River Zen at its best.

The navigable portion of the Blackwater River is 31 miles long. Numerous access points enable the paddler to easily pick and choose desired sections. Not surprisingly, the upper river is narrower with high banks and swift current, requiring more expertise. The lower river is generally suited for beginners. Primitive camping is allowed on sandbars along the river, and Blackwater River State Park has a full-service campground. The nearest towns of any size are Milton, about 15 miles to the west, and Crestview, about the same distance to the east.

Other scenic rivers in the Blackwater region and drainage include Juniper Creek, Shoal River, and the Yellow River. Red Rock Bridge, near the beginning of Juniper Creek, is believed to be the location of where General Andrew Jackson crossed with his troops and Creek Indian allies during the First Seminole War of 1817–1818 when Florida was still claimed by Spain. Jackson sought to punish the Seminole Indians and recapture escaped slaves who sought refuge with the Seminoles. Juniper Creek boasts sand bluffs and mountain laurel, and one can either paddle the waterway or hike along it on the Florida National Scenic Trail—or do both in one outing as a shuttle alternative.

The Shoal River is another short run with gold-tinted water and sandy shores, while the Yellow River is much longer with faster current, draining the state's highest elevations. The river begins in Alabama and runs about 100 miles before emptying into Blackwater Bay. Water levels can fluctuate rapidly. While the upper sections can be ideal for paddling if not in flood stage, the lower sections are suitable for motorboats.

NEW

North Florida's New River is like no other swamp stream. It emerges from swamps, gets lost in a swamp, and then flows through one of Florida's most famous swamps as it snakes its way 37 miles to the Gulf. The river's upper section courses through stands of cypress and stately Atlantic white cedar in the Apalachicola National Forest, although numerous snags make it difficult to navigate. At one point, the river widens as it enters Mud Swamp, part of the 8,090-acre Mud Swamp/New River Wilderness Area, providing the illusion of a navigable stream. This wide channel is short-lived, however, because the river abruptly fans out into several impassable channels. Only near the bottom of the wilderness area does the river re-form again and begin flowing through the famed Tate's Hell Swamp.

Tate's Hell was named for Cebe Tate, who became lost for seven days in the 200,000-acre morass in 1875 while hunting a panther. When he crawled out onto a Carrabelle street, hungry and snake-bitten, someone asked him where he had been, and he murmured, "My name is Cebe Tate, and I just came from hell!"

The New River, while remote and wild, can be the setting for a lovely paddling trip through Tate's Hell if the water is high enough, with twisted cypress roots and knees and gnarly tupelo gum trees to behold. And the Tate's Hell State Forest offers several scenic riverside campsites, ideal for planning an overnight trip.

Another river in Tate's Hell is quite different. The Crooked River, a 25-mile blackwater stream, roughly parallels the Gulf Coast and is tidally influenced at both ends with the narrowest section in the middle. Navigable throughout its length, the Crooked River connects to the short Carrabelle River on the western end and to the lower Ochlockonee River at the eastern terminus. Like the New River, the Florida Forest Service has set up primitive campsites along its shores, and the wild region is a haven for the Florida black bear.

OCHLOCKONEE

Emerging from fertile farmlands north of Thomasville and Moultrie, Georgia, the Ochlockonee River has a dual personality: it is either challenging to navigate due to frequent logjams at low water, or it is a dangerous roller coaster at high water. In the middle section, the river is interrupted by Lake Talquin and the Jackson Bluff Dam before continuing through some of the wildest forest lands in the state.

Emerging from the dam, the Ochlockonee gives the appearance of a wide, easy-flowing river, but it quickly narrows and becomes fast and tortuous in sections, with numerous side streams and sloughs. In places there are bluffs and long sandbars, and in others, thick river swamps dominated by cypress and tupelo gum trees with little dry land. Near the Gulf, the river widens and flows past vast salt marsh prairies and mazes of tidal creeks.

It is no surprise that Paddle Florida, which organizes trips for 30 to 60 people, chose the Ochlockonee as their featured Northwest Florida river for several annual six-day "Dam to the Bay" adventures. The river below the dam has all the elements for a perfect group trip—wildness and conveniently spaced group campgrounds. On a typical morning, with the waterway cloaked in a rising mist, a bald eagle would be perched in a tall snag, while otters playfully romped along the shore and great blue herons flew overhead. During the trip, paddlers would spot various ducks, alligators, turtles, water snakes, wild turkeys, woodpeckers, wading birds, and graceful swallow-tailed kites. Plants, too, would put on a show along the river as spring unfolded with each day—bright green cypress needles and gum

Paddling the Ochlockonee River in spring.

I sometimes took friends along to explore my secret world at the Ochlockonee's edge. Like Indiana Jones's lost tombs, at low water the river swamp would reveal giant cathedral rooms with white sand floors and high ceilings formed by the green leafy canopy. . . . The highest part of the river's ceiling was always moving with birds and climbing animals. We enjoyed visiting a place we called "the center of the earth," a wild refuge completely hidden by thick, almost impenetrable walls of green poison ivy and cat claw thorns. Years later, in college, I read the accounts of great naturalists like Bartram, Thoreau, and Burroughs and felt a powerful and even spiritual connection to them, recalling my small river swamp ramblings. These were the beginnings of my quest for a life as a modern-day naturalist.

—JOHN M. HALL, WRITING IN THE *BETWEEN TWO RIVERS* ANTHOLOGY (CERULEAN ET AL., EDS.)

leaves, red maple seeds, striking redbud trees, and the fragrant white and pink blossoms of wild azalea.

On the challenging side, the river would sometimes flood during a Paddle Florida trip, sending someone scurrying back by vehicle to Ed and Bernice's Fish Camp along Highway 20 with everyone's keys in order to move vehicles out of low-lying areas. Several vehicles narrowly have escaped being inundated with rising waters. Sudden spring floods are a common occurrence on the Ochlockonee.

Before the modern kayaker and canoeist, mostly anglers knew the Ochlockonee, fishing either along shore or in wooden "jon boats." The original jon boats were often made from cypress boards with pine pitch covering the seams. And before motors, anglers used wooden paddles to power these boats, often sculling up or down the river.

G. M. Rogers, writing in *Florida Wildlife* magazine in 1994, recalled these early fishing days on the river:

I have vivid memories of women, cane poles on their shoulders, walking the sandy roads down to the river where they would fish, eat dinner and sing songs. Their catch of the day most likely included channel catfish, as well as red-bellied bream, which were carried home in burlap bags called "croaker sacks."

The bream angler's tackle was more often than not a stubbed off cane pole—short so it would stay stiff—with good, heavy line. The men (and women, because this was also a women's pastime) would drop "gator fleas," wild crickets, and red wigglers deep between the logjams and jerk out the big bream. No one had coolers or live wells—just six-foot stringers. A person could have a tough time lifting out a six-foot stringer full of river bream!

Paddlers make their way up Mack Slough along the Ochlockonee River.

Sunrise paddlers on the lower Ochlockonee River.

A Red-bellied Watersnake in a cypress slough along the river.

Ecologically, the Ochlockonee is home to several threatened and endangered mussels that include the purple bankclimber, oval pigtoe, Ochlockonee moccasinshell, Gulf moccasinshell, and Ochlockonee arcmussel. Mussels are a key indicator of a river's health, and the southeastern United States harbors almost 90 percent of the freshwater mussels in the United States. Sixty species of mussels and clams are found in Florida, and most of these thrive in waters west of the Suwannee River in rivers such as the Ochlockonee.

SOPCHOPPY

The upper Sopchoppy River is one of Florida's true wild and scenic rivers, although lacking in official designation. The upper reaches emerge from the vast swamps and piney woods of the Apalachicola National Forest, with the largest swamp being the 24,600-acre Bradwell Bay Wilderness Area. As it courses through the coastal plain, the river has sculpted steep sand bluffs and exposed cypress roots and buttresses. To glide down the red-black water—golden when seen against a white sand bank—is truly a pleasure under the right conditions.

In spring, the Sopchoppy River is one of the best showcases for wildflowers. A great profusion of wild azaleas bloom along the shorelines, some with almost pure white blossoms and others revealing a deep pink. They smell like honeysuckle, much sweeter than the nonnative azaleas seen in landscaped environments.

Along the Sopchoppy, especially on the five-mile stretch from Mt. Beasor Church Bridge to the city park in Sopchoppy, brilliant white fringe trees bloom along with red trumpet flowers on vine-wrapped branches and tree trunks. In the wetter places, Southern blue flag irises draw attention along with spider lilies with their drooping white petals. In addition, all the shoreline trees pop out in various shades of brilliant green. The river's dark waters are a perfect mirror for their emergence, and for the slow paddler, the beauty has a way of seeping inside.

Of course, wildlife is active along the river in all seasons. Red-shouldered hawks call noisily over the tannin waters, and paddlers along the watercourse are serenaded by a great variety of songbirds. If one is quiet, deer can sometimes be seen drinking in the shallows, and on warm days turtles, snakes, and the occasional alligator are often sunning on logs, branches, and sandbars. Paddling quietly in a kayak or canoe is a great way to experience the seasons along the Sopchoppy, although there is also a scenic stretch of the Florida National Scenic Trail along the river on Apalachicola National Forest lands.

Spring is when the annual Worm Grunting Festival is held near the river in downtown Sopchoppy. Music, crafts, and, of course, worm grunting demonstrations are all featured. To "grunt" for worms, you first take a stob or post and pound it in the ground and rub the top with a flat piece of iron to create a vibration and grunting sound. This is supposed to sound like a hungry burrowing mole and the native earthworms—*Diplocardia mississippiensis* to be exact—flee to the surface for self-protection. They are then gathered for freshwater fish bait.

Sopchoppy River reflections in the Apalachicola National Forest.

Wild azaleas in bloom along the Sopchoppy River.

The most scenic part of the Sopchoppy any time of year is the upper portion in the Apalachicola National Forest, but water levels should be between 9 and 11 feet at the online U.S. Geological Survey (USGS) 02327100 Sopchoppy gauge for ideal paddling conditions. If the river is too low, sandbars and snags will require negotiating; too high, and you'll be paddling into branches at a swift speed. These upper reaches have high banks and sandbars, and the river twists around a myriad of cypress knees and artistically exposed roots. And being in the national forest, there is no human development—only wild river.

A few hardy souls tackle the upper reaches by launching at Forest Highway 13 and paddling six tortuous miles to Forest Road 346. I tried this once with family members in two canoes, and we spent most of the day pulling over snags. Afterward, we could truly say it was a wilderness paddling experience.

A more doable section is to launch at Forest Road 329 and paddle three miles to the Oak Park Cemetery

Bridge or paddle onward another five miles to the Mt. Beasor Church Bridge or ten miles to the Hodge City Park in downtown Sopchoppy, for a total of thirteen miles. The last few miles are scenic, but riverside houses are present. The Forest Service roads are unpaved, so they may be sloppy after large rain events, and some of the launches are steep and sandy. Below Sopchoppy, the river gradually widens for 10 miles until it merges with the Ochlockonee River at Ochlockonee River State Park. The lower river is suitable for motorboats, but the upper river is only passable by kayak or canoe at the right water levels.

AUCILLA AND BIG BEND STREAMS

Florida's rivers are unique in many respects, especially those that swirl underground before reaching the Gulf or Atlantic. The Aucilla is one of these disappearing rivers, the land having opened up and swallowed the winding blackwater stream hundreds or even thousands of years ago. But after the river disappears, it pops up and disappears again about thirty times in an area known as the Aucilla Sinks, a great place to hike.

The reason for all of this fickleness is karst, a limestone base that is porous, having been eroded by water over time. The result is sinkholes that open up and swallow land into underground caverns. Many of the Aucilla sinkholes have flow, while others are more stagnant, as if occurring along river oxbows. And they have unique beauty. Cypress, gum, live oak, and maple frame steep banks of dark limestone that contain the river flow. Some sinks are a quarter-mile long. The river emerges at one end and sinks again at the other, while other sinks are only small windows into the subterranean depths with little or no apparent current.

The Aucilla sinks are also windows into the past. Some of Florida's oldest human artifacts have been found in its sinks, left during a time when the water table was much lower and the deep sinks may have been the only reliable places for both people and animals to obtain fresh water. They were also hunting sites for Paleo peoples 12,000 to 15,000 years ago when mammoths, mastodons, giant sloths, and saber-toothed tigers roamed the land.

S. David Webb was one of the first trained archaeologists to probe the depths of "Booger Hole" (now the Page/Ladson Site) near the middle of the Aucilla's Half Mile Rise, a spot where the underground river rises to the surface for about a half-mile. On the second dive of the fourth day, he found a mammoth radius bone that appeared to have been worn down on one side and snapped off about two-thirds of the

One of the Aucilla River's many sinks.

Aucilla River reflections.

The Aucilla River is also known for the Big Rapids, a thrill for canoeists and kayakers.

way down. It was then that he had an epiphany: "At that moment a curtain of silt obscured my view," he wrote in the anthology, *Between Two Rivers* (Cerulean et al., eds.):

> As I stared intently, waiting for the water to clear, a vision of a woman emerged from the darkness. She picked up an intact mammoth radius bone and began scraping a hide. She yelled strange sounds to a child seated nearby. Then she gave a hard thrust to the radius and I saw it snap. The longer piece fell to the ground; she stared at the distal end remaining in her hand. Even as I squinted in the back-scattered light to take in more of this scene, the woman and child faded into the darkness of the river sediments, and I was left astonished, cradling that same bone in my hands.

Over the next several years, the underwater excavation of the Aucilla River's artifact-rich sinkhole was known as "the stairway into the past."

Besides the Aucilla, Florida's Big Bend region has several other swamp-fed blackwater streams. They include the Econfina, Fenholloway, Steinhatchee, and Waccasassa, all of them shorter than the 89-mile Aucilla. Both the Econfina and Fenholloway Rivers emerge from the 25,000-acre San Pedro Swamp, but their historic paths diverge significantly. The Econfina, often confused with the spring-fed stream by the same name above Panama City, primarily flows through undeveloped land and is generally impassable until it reaches U.S. Highway 98/19. Then, only an experienced canoeist or kayaker at higher water levels should attempt to paddle the eight twisting miles through Econfina River State Park, occasionally pulling over downed trees. The area was the site of a running battle in 1818 during the First Seminole War when Andrew Jackson invaded Spanish Florida in an effort to punish Seminoles and capture escaped slaves.

The Fenholloway flows through Perry and is the longtime recipient of effluent from a paper mill. Designated as Florida's only industrial river by the 1947 Florida Legislature, allowing it to be legally polluted, the effluent will soon be piped directly to the Gulf of Mexico, bypassing most of the river. Visually, the Fenholloway is a wild-looking, undeveloped waterway with a rich history where wealthy northerners stayed at the renowned Hampton Springs Lodge, having come south for fishing, hunting, sightseeing, and soaking in the mineral-laden waters of Hampton Springs just off the main river. Theodore Roosevelt was the lodge's most famous visitor. The lodge burned down in 1954, the same year the paper mill was constructed along the Fenholloway.

The Steinhatchee River emerges as a narrow stream from Mallory Swamp, picking up several tributaries before

Cheyenne Alderson running the Big Rapids in a kayak at higher water.

Sunset along the Aucilla River near where some of Florida's oldest human artifacts have been found.

swirling underground near U.S. 98 at Tennille. Soon after resurfacing, the river dramatically flows over a rock ledge—Steinhatchee Falls—an area long occupied by Native Americans. The river then flows another six miles through largely state-owned land before passing the recreational fishing haven of Steinhatchee and emptying into the Gulf.

The Waccasassa River flows through one of Florida's most remote regions, the Waccasassa Bay Preserve State Park, primarily an area of marsh, tree islands, and oyster bars. The river originates from both springs and a swamp known as Devil's Hammock. The snag-prone section above U.S. 19 is where the Wild Hog Canoe Race is held every spring, advertised as a challenging obstacle course courtesy of Mother Nature where participants must lift, push, drag, wade, swim, and occasionally paddle for a grueling 15 miles, meeting reptilian river creatures along the way. It is a charity fundraiser. Most sane paddlers and boaters launch at a ramp below U.S. 19 and follow the gentle river four miles to Waccasassa Bay and its many tidal creeks.

OCKLAWAHA

The Ocklawaha River has a storied past, from being a point of conflict during the Second Seminole War to facing near annihilation from the Cross Florida Barge Canal.

It was at Payne's Landing along the Ocklawaha that some Seminole chiefs were coerced into signing a treaty in 1832 to move their people to present-day Oklahoma. Many Seminoles rejected the treaty, including Osceola, the war leader. He allegedly plunged a knife into the treaty, declaring, "The only treaty I will ever execute will be this!"

Some of those chiefs who tried to move West were killed. In one incident, Osceola sprinkled the body of Charley Emathla with the gold coins Emathla had received for agreeing to move. Previously, Seminoles occupied much of the Ocklawaha region as part of the Treaty of Moultrie Creek only nine years earlier, but when Andrew Jackson became president, he had other ideas. He wanted to rid Florida and the rest of the Southeast of all Native Americans.

After the Seminoles were driven to the Everglades region or sent to Oklahoma as a result of years of warfare, steamboats began chugging up the Ocklawaha to Silver Springs as part of a burgeoning tourist trade. Sidney Lanier, writing about a steamboat ride up the river in the early 1870s, described the Ocklawaha as

1902 photo of a ferry taking a wagon across the Ocklawaha River. DETROIT PHOTOGRAPHIC CO.

the sweetest water-lane in the world, a lane which runs for more than a hundred and fifty miles of pure delight betwixt hedgerows of oaks and cypresses and palms and bays and magnolias and mosses and manifold vine-growths, a lane clean to travel along for there is never a speck of dust in it save the blue dust and gold dust which the wind blows out of the flags and lilies, a lane which is as if a typical woods-stroll had taken shape and as if God had turned into water and trees the recollection of some meditative ramble through the lonely seclusions of His own soul.

Journalist George M. Barbour accompanied Ulysses Grant on an all-night steamboat trip up the Ocklawaha to the spring in 1880. "These covered passages are solemn and impressive at any time; but in the night, when lighted up by the blaze of the brilliant bonfire burning on the roof of the wheel-house, then the scene is quite indescribable," he wrote in *Florida for Tourists, Invalids and Settlers.* "The inky water, the lights and shadows of the foliage, the disturbed birds as they wheel gracefully out of sight, all leave an impression never to be forgotten."

It is a wonderful revelation to a visitor from the North to make a trip on one of Florida's tropical rivers. None is more interesting than the Ocklawaha, which for scores of miles contorts and intorts its way through the tangled growth of pristine forests, all the while seeking a lower level, until at last it pours its clear flood in the murky waters of the broad and imposing St. John's at Welaka. It may be that the Ocklawaha originally intended to be straight, but, if so, it does it by a most wonderful series of windings and contortions. "On the Ocklawaha"—there is euphony in the name alone. Had we but a fraction of the rhythm of the ancient Indians who bestowed the names upon Florida's lakes and rivers, the decadence of poetry in this country need not be deplored.

—NEVIN O. WINTER, *FLORIDA, THE LAND OF ENCHANTMENT,* 1918

Above: A notched cypress log along the Ocklawaha River, likely made by early loggers.
Below: The Ocklawaha River near Orange Springs.

Swamp maple seeds, a sign of early spring along Florida rivers.

Steamboat passengers found great sport in shooting alligators and other creatures from the boat decks until steamboat captains put a stop to the practice. The wildlife that people came to see was dwindling, partly due to the free-wheeling shooters. Loggers began cutting the cypress and other trees from the floodplain and hauling them out by log rafts or by dragging them through the swamps by cables to tram railway cars. Still, the Ocklawaha and its many side streams and swamps were remote places, ideal for a flourishing moonshine industry for several decades. Marjorie Kinnan Rawlings immortalized the practice in her novel, *South Moon Under*, published in 1932.

Then came one of the most grandiose engineering dreams in Florida history—the Cross Florida Barge Canal. Decades in the making, and started and stopped a couple of times, the canal dammed part of the lower Ocklawaha, flooding 14,000 acres of floodplain and several springs. The entire river would have been ditched if President Richard Nixon had not halted the project in 1971. Even most of the Silver River would have been flooded. "The purpose of the canal was to reduce transportation costs for barge shipping," President Nixon said when executing his order.

It was conceived and designed at a time when the focus of Federal concern in such matters was still almost completely on maximizing economic return. In calculating that return, the destruction of natural, ecological values was not counted as a cost, nor was a credit allowed for actions preserving the environment. A natural treasure is involved in the case of the Barge Canal—the Oklawaha River—a uniquely beautiful, semitropical stream, one of a very few of its kind in the United States, which would be destroyed by construction of the Canal.

Land for the canal was given to the state of Florida, and eventually the 110-mile long Cross Florida Greenway was created as a recreation and wildlife corridor.

While most of the Ocklawaha River was spared, the Rodman Dam still blocks the river and backs up water in the Rodman Reservoir. Migratory fish and manatees are impeded, along with paddlers and boaters. During periodic drawdowns, several clear springs reappear in the exposed lake bottom and alongside creeks, and this excites activists who seek to remove Rodman Dam and restore the middle portion of the river. The dam issue has been a flashpoint for decades, and even though several Florida governors have supported dam

Several springs along the Ocklawaha were flooded when the Rodman Dam was built, including Cannon Springs. This is the scenic opening to the spring.

removal, the dam remains due to a lack of political will in the Florida Legislature.

For the paddler and boater, the Ocklawaha River from the Silver River confluence to the Ocklawaha Canoe Outpost Resort is the most popular section. Most launch at Ray Wayside Park, run by Marion County, just off State Road 40. Since much of the shoreline is managed by the Cross Florida Greenway or the U.S. Forest Service, the river is strikingly beautiful and usually tannin-tinted, depending on rainfall. An occasional snag is present during low water levels, so inquire about river conditions at the Ocklawaha Canoe Outpost before embarking.

The county-run Gore's Landing, about 10 miles below Ray, is a great place to camp, with restrooms and cold showers. The large live oaks that canopy the campground are festooned with epiphytes and bromeliads. From Gore's Landing, it is just over 9 miles to the Ocklawaha Canoe Outpost Resort where you can camp or rent charming cedar cabins. Be sure to check out the resort's giant mulberry tree, one of the largest in the state.

Below the canoe outpost, the river gradually widens and the current slows as the effects of the Rodman Dam take hold. Cannon Springs, about five miles below the outpost on river right, can be reached at the end of a canopied side channel. The spring may or may not be clear, depending on the water level. During periodic reservoir drawdowns, the spring boil usually reappears and is a popular destination for paddlers.

If paddling or boating below Cannon Springs, the river widens into a broad path of cypress and waterweeds. In fall, yellow marsh marigolds cover vast areas in meadow-like beauty. The challenge here can be floating tussocks of water lettuce that clog the channel, so reaching the landing at Orange Springs can be difficult. On the first Paddle Florida trip down the river in 2016, a Florida Park Service airboat with a scoop rake attached to the front had to repeatedly clear a path for the 60 or so paddlers. Periodic drawdowns and spraying help to reduce the abundance of water lettuce, although the long-disputed Rodman Dam is the ultimate culprit.

If paddling or boating through the Rodman Reservoir, be sure to follow the channel markers because to do otherwise can land you in a forest of stumps from when the land was cleared for the reservoir. Efforts are being made to build an easy portage site around the dam for paddlers who want to continue on the natural river channel. Below the dam, the river winds another 13 miles through unspoiled floodplain until it empties into the St. Johns River. The takeout is across the St. Johns at the town of Welaka. Despite the impediment of the dam and reservoir, much of the Ocklawaha is worthy of exploration just as it was during the steamboat days.

ST. MARYS

Snaking its way along the Florida and Georgia border, the slow-moving St. Marys River emerges from the massive Okefenokee Swamp and twists 130 miles to the Cumberland Sound and Atlantic Ocean near Fernandina. Largely undeveloped, white sandbars contrast with tea-colored water that is framed by large hardwood trees. Known for scenic paddling and bream and bass fishing, rare fish species include the blackbanded sunfish and banded topminnow.

The St. Marys River and Okefenokee Swamp was the home of some of the earliest American pioneers, and there was even a battle along its shore between Georgia colonists and British soldiers during the American Revolution. To better understand how these early pioneers lived in the Okefenokee headwaters area, visitors can tour Obediah's Okefenok, a re-creation of Obediah Barber's 1800s homestead. Exhibits include a cabin, barn, blacksmith shop, smoke house, potato house, and sugarcane mill. Visitors can also tour a similar homestead in the Okefenokee National Wildlife Refuge.

The rich history of the St. Marys and Okefenokee spawned ghostly tales told for generations. "One tale has it that on stormy nights the ghost of a slave ship— La Estrellita—sails up the St. Mary's River, a prong that extends into the swamp," wrote Cecile Hulse Matschat in *Suwannee River: Strange Green Land* in 1938. "She is manned by the skeletons of long-dead seamen, who abandon their contraband cargo on the hidden islands. The clanking of slave chains can be heard clearly on still nights!"

In reality, the great swamp was once a refuge for runaway slaves and Civil War deserters, and it is now a haven for nature lovers. While much of the river and its headwaters swamp are remote and wild, in 2020 the national organization American Rivers named the St. Marys River and Okefenokee Swamp as among America's "Most Endangered Rivers" due to proposed titanium stripmining in the region, which could encompass thousands of acres. "The St. Marys is an extraordinarily beautiful and fragile blackwater river that has shaped the history, economy, and culture of our region," said Alex Kearns of the St. Marys

The Chesser Family homestead, part of the St. Marys River headwaters in the Okefenokee National Wildlife Refuge.

Earthkeepers in response to the mining threats. "It is essential, irreplaceable and cherished."

TOMOKA AND NEARBY STREAMS

Much has been written about the Tomoka River and its native inhabitants through the centuries. Spanish explorers in the early 1600s stopped at the Timucua village of Nocoroco where the Tomoka meets the Halifax River, a coastal lagoon now part of the Intracoastal Waterway. The Spanish described everything about the Timucua, from their houses, forts, foods, burial practices, and even their appearance—mostly tall and tawny and covered with tattoos. Clothing was mostly deerskin and Spanish moss. Now preserved in Tomoka State Park, what remains of Nocoroco are 40-foot-tall shell middens made from decades of discarded shells from Native American meals.

When the Timucua were largely killed off by disease and warfare, large plantations were established in the region, growing mostly cotton and indigo. When these faded, tour boats in the late 1800s began taking tourists up the Tomoka River to see a slice of wild Florida. Nevin O. Winter wrote about a steamboat excursion up the river in his 1918 travel guide *Florida, The Land of Enchantment*, an account that rings true today:

> From its mouth the river very slowly winds inland in long and easy curves, and is confined within wooded banks. It is generally a narrow stream, and the swash of the waters will be heard along the shore as the little boat pushes its way along. An occasional alligator will be sighted along the bank, for this is one of the streams in which these ugly creatures are found. As the boat ascends, the river becomes attenuated and vegetation becomes more and more of a tangle, as well as more tropical. Palmettos and live oaks overhang the banks, while the dark waters flow sluggishly along underneath. The variety of coloring in the vegetation is unusual and astonishing to one who is making his first trip to this semi-tropical land.

Today, the Tomoka is a scenic, mostly undeveloped 20-mile waterway and canopied in the upper reaches. One can easily motor or paddle upstream from two launch points—at the state park and at the Tomoka

Buckhead Bluff, on the Tomoka River near Ormond, Fla.

Above: A postcard of Buckhead Bluff along the Tomoka River, postmarked 1907. HUGH C. LEIGHTON CO. OF PORTLAND, MAINE, MADE IN GERMANY
Below: Kayakers on the Tomoka River in Tomoka River State Park.

Estates Boat Ramp just outside the park. Since these launch sites are at the bottom of the river, it is a long journey to the top and back for a paddler, so a motorboat is perhaps the best way to see the entire waterway. Another option would be to commission a motorboat to act as a "mother ship" to take kayaks or canoes near the top and drop them off for a leisurely downstream paddle of several miles.

Other notable blackwater streams in the area include Bulow Creek. Only a few miles in length, the stream runs through Bulow Plantation Ruins State Park, once a prosperous plantation that grew sugarcane, cotton, rice, and indigo. It was destroyed by Seminole Indians during the Second Seminole War. Today, ruins of the former sugar mill and crumbling foundations of buildings can be seen. Like many streams in this region, Bulow Creek spills out into the Intracoastal Waterway.

Pellicer Creek is another short, calm waterway. It winds through the unspoiled forests of Faver-Dykes State Park and the 1,500-acre Princess Place Preserve, managed by Flagler County. Formerly called Woodcutters Creek, the waterway once carried timber and turpentine from a mill to the Mantanzas River and onward to St. Augustine. The creek was later renamed for an area plantation owner, Francisco Pellicer.

Spruce Creek, a few miles below the Tomoka River, was once the site of a large Timucua Indian ceremonial and political center. Prehistoric Timucua earthworks, the Spruce Creek Mound, are located along the creek.

ECONLOCKHATCHEE

The Econlockhatchee River, Econ for short, is a blackwater river flowing through largely undeveloped lands just east of Orlando. Many of the banks are tall and handsome, arching live oaks and palms form a shaded canopy in places, and numerous wading birds and alligators grace the shorelines. What more can you ask from a wild river?

In summer, like some other central Florida blackwater rivers, the Econ is prone to fish kills. Two primary culprits cause most fish kills: blue-green algae blooms and low dissolved oxygen. Fish need to "breathe" just as land animals, but instead of using lungs, they absorb oxygen gases (dissolved oxygen) in the water through their gills.

Harmful algae blooms can be caused by warm weather combined with runoff and discharges from septic tanks, human development, farms, and other land-use activities that raise nitrogen and phosphorous levels in the water. Large algae blooms can block sunlight, often killing rooted water plants that are valuable fish habitat and reducing oxygen levels in the water. Some types of algae can be toxic to humans as well as to fish.

Low levels of dissolved oxygen in water can also be caused by high temperatures and low water levels because hot water holds less oxygen than cold water. Even extended periods of cloudy weather and high rainfall can cause fish kills because the system uses up oxygen faster than it is generated without the sun helping to produce oxygen. Plus, rainfall can flush organic materials such as grass clippings and leaves into the water and when these decompose, more oxygen is used up. So, some fish kills can occur due to both human activities and natural weather patterns, or a combination of both. But don't let that dissuade you from exploring the wild Econ River.

WITHLACOOCHEE SOUTH

Withlacoochee means "little great water" or "little river" in the Muscogee/Seminole tongue.

Limpkins are not always common on Florida rivers, but the northwest-flowing Withlacoochee River near Dunnellon in east-central Florida is a modern-day limpkin haven. Around most bends, limpkins are probing, eating, and calling. Part of this bonanza is due to an invasion of nonnative apple snails that have increased their food supply.

One bit of warning. Limpkins have a screeching wake-up call in the wee hours. Roosters don't hold a candle to limpkins. The brown-and-white speckled birds are aptly named "the crying bird," and at four in the morning, they are the devil's alarm clock. According to limpkin expert Dana Bryan, night-calling limpkins are likely unattached males seeking the company of a female since unattached females often fly along the river at night during mating season. If they don't get lucky, they keep calling, and calling. It is like crooning all night at a maiden's window, but the beautiful damsel never invites you in.

Perhaps Seminole warriors could imitate the limpkin's mournful cry. Osceola's war cry was said to have elicited spine-tingling chills. In fact, his name meant "Black Drink Singer," someone who plays an important part in the annual Green Corn Ceremony, so he must have had a voice for song, and for war cries. Though not a designated chief, Osceola was in his prime during battles along the Withlacoochee, and he became a respected war leader.

Above: A limpkin with apple snail. The Withlacoochee River South is known for its large limpkin population.
Below: A female limpkin with chick.

Several skirmishes were fought along the river, the first when General Duncan Clinch came to the river with 750 men on New Year's Eve in 1835 in an attempt to drive Seminoles from the area. The ultimate goal was to remove the Indians from Florida to make room for white settlement, and to recapture escaped slaves. Clinch was unaware of what had befallen Major Francis Dade three days earlier, when Seminoles killed the major and more than a hundred of his men in a four-hour battle along the military road between Fort Brooke and Fort King—Florida's version of Custer at the Little Big Horn. The 100-mile road ran along the western boundary of the Seminole stronghold known as the Cove of the Withlacoochee. The Cove, now called Lake Tsala Apopka, consists of thick hammocks and swamps and a string of lakes, islands, and peninsulas. The Withlacoochee River arches around the Cove's eastern and northern borders, flowing north, not south.

Clinch, like most American generals, believed the Seminoles were divided by infighting, unable to muster a large capable fighting force. At a deep, swift point along the river, he and his men found a leaky dugout and began crossing seven and eight men at a time. The Seminoles, thinking Clinch would cross at a shallow ford a few miles downstream, quickly moved upstream by land to set up an ambush.

Clinch's regulars crossed first—about 250 in all—leaving a few hundred Florida Militia members along the western shore, their tours of duty set to expire the next day. The regulars moved about 150 yards inland to a clearing surrounded by a dense hammock and took a rest break. John Bemrose, an enlisted soldier in the outfit, described what happened next:

> An officer, Capt. [Charles] Mellon, was the first to discern an Indian skulking in the thicket and having obtained permission of his battalion colonel to fire, which he had not sooner done than it was answered by the peeling [sic] sound of 1000 rifles fired amidst the troops simultaneously, followed by the unearthly war whoop from a thousand savage throats. The suddenness of the thing, conjoined to the terrible and bloodcurdling cry of the Indians, struck at once terror and some degree of panic among the soldiers, and they retreated precipitously to where the surgeons were placed, leaving about 20 of their comrades weltering in their blood.

Several officers were quickly shot—a Seminole tactic—increasing the level of confusion.

The one-armed Colonel Alexander Fanning appealed to Clinch for permission to charge the hammock with bayonets. Clinch turned him down twice but, as described by Bemrose, Fanning made a third appeal, tears in his eyes: "General, my men will all be cut down. Oh, let me charge and my life for it, they will run!" The subsequent charge, and two others, may have saved Clinch's force from annihilation and allowed the force to retreat to the river. A makeshift bridge was created, and the regulars moved to the northern shore, carrying 59 wounded with them. Four had lost their lives. The death toll would have been higher had the Seminoles used larger-bore rifles. Seminole leaders claimed their casualties were three killed and five wounded.

Clinch retreated north to Fort Drane, realizing the Seminoles would not be easily uprooted from the Cove. Osceola sent a chilling letter to Clinch: "You have guns and so have we. . . . You have powder and lead, and so have we. . . . Your men will fight, and so will ours, till the last drop of Seminole's blood has moistened the dust of his hunting ground."

Ironically, Clinch was later called "Old Withlacoochee" in a run for Georgia governor, having somehow turned his retreat into victory in a way only skilled politicians can accomplish.

The Cove came under attack again that February when General Edmund Gaines and nearly a thousand men—with scant rations—repeatedly attempted to cross the Withlacoochee to round up the Seminoles. Seminole snipers repelled the troops, and Gaines retreated to the northern shore, but instead of leaving the area like Clinch, Gaines built a log fortification he named Camp Izard in honor of a fallen soldier. His plan was to draw in the entire Seminole fighting force of about 1,100 warriors so that when Clinch arrived with reinforcements, they could finish them off. The first part of Gaines's plan worked perfectly—he was soon surrounded on three sides. But where was Clinch?

At one point, Black and Indian warriors started a brush fire that raced down toward the fortress. They attacked from behind the smoke screen. Abruptly, the wind shifted; fire swept back on the warriors. They hastily retreated. A long siege ensued.

Lieutenant Henry Prince described one skirmish in his diary (*Amidst a Storm of Bullets*, Frank Laumer, ed.) that revealed the weakness of their breastworks:

> Whang! Whang! Pop! Fit! Whirr! Bang! Spatter! . . . I ran to my line company amidst a storm of bullets. The Indians were round us as represented by the dots. There were at least 1000. They kept at a long distance. The fight was a very smart one for 3 hours.

. . . It seems to me impossible for bullets to fly thicker anywhere then they did round me. They would cut holes through the palmetto leaves 3 feet from us while others would fall dead all round me. I was hit by two spent balls one in the hip and one in the back.

One rifle ball knocked out two of General Gaines's teeth. The soldiers built the breastworks higher.

Days passed. Gaines sent desperate appeals to Clinch at Fort Drane, but Clinch was torn between conflicting orders from Gaines—commander of the western

Scene along the Withlacoochee River South.

Gaines's distant cannons—but before receiving his reply, an impatient Clinch left with 500 men to rescue Gaines.

With scant supplies and Seminole snipers picking off soldiers who ventured outside the log walls, Gaines's men were becoming weak, trying to live on small rations of butchered horses, mules, and dogs. Some Seminoles, sensing an opportunity, called for a parley. Not all Seminoles were in agreement with this move, initiated by the Black Seminole John Caesar, but Osceola stood by him. Negotiations began, and Gaines seemed agreeable to recommend that all Seminoles be left alone south and west of the Withlacoochee, although he knew it was unlikely that President Andrew Jackson would ever abide by such an agreement. The talks were cut short by the arrival of Clinch's troops, who immediately fired upon the Seminoles.

It is difficult to visualize the soldiers leaving the cramped enclosure after eight days. Many staggered. Some had to be carried. A few yelled and screamed as if they had gone mad. Several ate food so quickly they became violently ill.

Long before the Seminole war battles, Hernando De Soto tromped through in 1539 in search of adventure and gold. Spanish chain mail was found in a nearby shell mound along the river. A branch of the Timucua tribe lived here for millennia until war and European-introduced disease took their tolls.

Still living along the river are centuries-old bald cypress trees that once towered over both Timucua and Seminole Indians paddling the river. Living history landmarks. Most are hollow, yet living, thus the reason early loggers spared them. Another feature of the river that hearkens back to the early days are the bird numbers. Large flocks of great egrets and white ibis are often seen.

A worthwhile side trip is to paddle up canopied Gum Slough. The four-mile waterway can be an obstacle course of rocks and logs, but the reward is a series of clear springs to explore. Along the shore are blooming red cardinal flowers, yellow bur marigolds, and blue flag irises. There are flocks of white ibis and, of course, limpkins. The slough is largely protected by the Half Moon–Gum Slough tract managed by the Water Management District, and the private landowner at the headsprings has signed a conservation easement, ensuring that the property will not be developed beyond personal dwellings.

The clear Rainbow River flows into the Withlacoochee at Dunnellon. From there, it flows a few more miles before widening into Lake Rousseau. Swallows,

forces—and General Winfield Scott—commander of the eastern forces. Gaines ordered Clinch to march immediately to his position along the Withlacoochee, while Scott ordered him to stay. By courier, Clinch pleaded with Scott to reconsider—he could hear

eagles, and ospreys often fill the skies, and countless American coots float on the water's surface. Numerous wading birds poke along grassy islands. Even a handful of royal terns can be seen perched on logs.

Lake Rousseau is one of Florida's oldest impounded lakes, dammed by the U.S. Department of the Army in 1909. A few years ago, 1,800 stumps were removed from the marked boating channels, but the lake's backwaters have ample long-lasting cypress stumps and wetland areas. Motorboat traffic is rare outside the marked channels, so it is a bird and paddler paradise. In one rookery area in the lake, 5,132 wading birds were counted around sunset. As with most rookeries, alligators help protect nesting birds from predators such as raccoons. Besides occasional disturbance by airboats and helicopters, the greatest threat to rookeries is significant water withdraws for human use.

A newer feature along the river is the Inglis Lock, part of the infamous Cross Florida Barge Canal. The dream of a canal bisecting Florida goes back to King Philip II of Spain in 1567. Rounding Florida was treacherous for his gold-bearing ships, as evidenced by the numerous shipwrecks along the east coast and in the Keys. U.S. Secretary of War John C. Calhoun revived the idea in 1818, again citing shipwrecks and also piracy, but the first dirt wasn't turned until the Great Depression when a sea-level canal was proposed, meaning that digging would need to go down more than 150 feet in central parts of the state. The project was canceled in 1942 over concerns about aquifer damage, but it was revived again in the 1960s with a design for several locks and dams. As noted in the Ocklawaha River discussion, after parts of the lower Withlacoochee and Ocklawaha Rivers were altered by canal construction, the project was halted by President Richard Nixon in 1971 as the nation's— and Florida's—environmental movement was gaining momentum and public support.

Today, the former canal lands are managed by the Florida Park Service. In a fitting tribute, the Cross Florida Greenway was named after the canal's chief opponent, Marjorie Harris Carr, while a dam on the lower Ocklawaha bears the name of a major canal proponent, former state senator George Kirkpatrick. I knew both in my early days of environmental lobbying. Carr was a raspy-voiced activist and skillful organizer, while Kirkpatrick had a sense of bravado, as evidenced by a large poster of a six-gun-carrying John Wayne greeting visitors in his Senate office. Today, the canal dream is dead, while more than 110 miles of hiking, biking, and multiuse trails are managed by the greenway. A debate

is still raging concerning the fate of the Kirkpatrick Dam and Rodman Reservoir along the lower Ocklawaha, while the much older Lake Rousseau Reservoir is less controversial, perhaps due to the large numbers of bird rookeries in the lake.

On one Paddle Florida camping trip along the Withlacoochee River, I opened my tent zipper in the morning and was showered with frost. My kayak sponge was frozen solid. Even in central Florida, February camping can be unpredictable, and we had likely experienced winter's coldest night. Maybe a little hardship is appropriate along a river where so many fought and died. The war cries and cannons have long been silent, but the results of the Withlacoochee battles and those that followed helped to shape Florida's future along with that of the Seminole Nation.

The Seminoles, like nearly all of America's native peoples, stood in the way of Manifest Destiny. Ultimately, the Cove of the Withlacoochee wasn't large enough to conceal them. Only the vast swamps of the Everglades and Big Cypress successfully shielded a few remnant Seminole bands and allowed them to remain on the land and in the waters they called home.

Slowly thawing, we ended our trip on the Withlacoochee by paddling through the towns of Inglis and Yankeetown, passing numerous shrimp boats and other ocean-going vessels. Mullet leaped and coastal cedars and palms were numerous. Sun felt warm on my face— the previous night's freeze almost forgotten—and the Seminole battle sites and limpkins were many miles upstream. The historic Withlacoochee River was emptying into the Gulf as it always had, and I felt freer for gliding along with her.

PITHLACHASCOTEE AND ANCLOTE

The Pithlachascotee is often called the 'Cotee River for short. The Pithlachascotee River emerges from Crews Lake and winds 23 miles to the Gulf of Mexico through several conservation areas, including the Starkey Wilderness Park and the Grey Preserve. In these upper reaches, live oaks form a shady canopy while sabal palms reach skyward. The river then flows through the town of New Port Richey before making its way to the Gulf of Mexico. Boating is popular in the river's lower reaches, while paddlers enjoy the narrow and shallow upper reaches. The long Seminole name of this river means "canoe building river," which is perhaps a reflection of the place where Seminole Indians chopped and dug out canoes from cypress and pine logs.

A Pithlachascotee River scene, just below the Grey Preserve.

The nearby Anclote River flows through Tarpon Springs, Florida's historic sponge fishing community. One can peruse the town's famous sponge docks and visit a small museum that describes the industry that was begun by Greek sponge divers in the late 1800s. The industry flourished until a blight decimated Gulf sponge beds in the 1940s. Sponging has since revived—sponge boats travel to and from the Gulf on the lower Anclote River—and Tarpon Springs is again a world leader in the natural sponge market.

Sponge Exchange in Tarpon Springs, circa 1915. HILLSBORO NEWS CO., TAMPA, FLORIDA

HILLSBOROUGH

The Hillsborough is a river of extremes. On one end is the 17 Runs, perhaps the most untamed section of river in the state where adventurers spend over six hours pulling kayaks or canoes over logs and trying to determine which channel might lead them out safely before dark. The other extreme is a wide waterway where city skyscrapers glitter on a dark mirror. Both segments are within 40 miles of each other.

The 54-mile Hillsborough emerges from central Florida's Green Swamp as does the Withlacoochee South, Alafia, Peace, and part of the Kissimmee River. The river can easily be divided into four distinct sections. Part of the upper river flows through Hillsborough River State Park and is the only river in peninsular Florida that has any real rapids. One can hike a trail to view them, as they are closed to boaters, but you can canoe or kayak an easy three-mile section nearby.

The park also features a reconstructed Second Seminole War–era fort. It was initially built to protect a strategic bridge over the Hillsborough River as part of a 100-mile military road. If the bridge was burned by Seminoles, it might take two days to portage wagons and supplies over the river. A cannon points across the bridge as it did in 1836.

The next river section is the innocent-sounding 17 Runs. A warning sign reads: "Give up all hope ye who enter here." Only five miles in length, it takes more than six hours to make one's way through the wilderness tangle of snags and confusing river braids. At low water levels, it is even confusing to determine the current's direction. Paddlers need to have excellent

The Hillsborough begins in the Green Swamp, nine hundred square miles of central Florida wilderness where white ibises drift in shadows over willow-bordered pools. From high water oaks great Spanish moss trails softly. The stillness is broken by the songs of Carolina wrens in the thickets, by the insistent voices of leopard frogs, by the calling of rain crows on slow summer afternoons.

—GLORIA JAHODA, *RIVER OF THE GOLDEN IBIS*

Above: White ibis along the Hillsborough River.
Below: A postcard of the Hillsboro River in Tampa, postmarked 1910. INTERNATIONAL POSTCARD CO., NEW YORK, MADE IN GERMANY

Hillsboro River, Tampa, Fla.

survival and orienteering skills. Inexperienced paddlers have had to be rescued by helicopter and presented with a bill afterwards.

The 17 Runs is not maintained due to manpower and cost but also to allow for advanced paddlers to experience a truly wild section of river where one is almost guaranteed not to see another human being. Two experienced paddlers, John and Beth Courtright, decided to tackle 17 Runs on an early May afternoon:

Four or so miles and several hours of daylight, what could go wrong? We answered this question as we proceeded down the river. Quickly we came upon our first portage. A tree lay across the water. We all exited and walked through the ankle-deep water to pull our kayaks over the log and settle back in to paddle. Unfortunately, we learned that paddling was out; we now were wet hiking with a kayak. The portages came one after the other, so frequently we opted to push our kayaks and swim behind them to the next obstructive log.

All fun during the daylight hours, soon we noted that the sun was setting. Our GPSs revealed that we had only paddled a small section and had miles to go. It dawned on all of us; we would soon be in the dark. Amongst the four of us we had one flashlight, so the leader got to hold it while the rest of us followed behind. On a positive note, not only was it a full moon, but actually a SUPER MOON.

Plunged into darkness, the trees became too large to simply step around or over. Our new method involved dragging ourselves onto large logs, pulling our kayaks over the log, and holding them in the current for re-entry. For the next few hours, this challenge continuously presented itself. No time for panic, just maintain a slow continuous progress down the river.

Eventually, the park rangers were able to track down our phone number and called to ascertain if we were lost or needed help. We later learned that many paddlers get lost on this section and end up spending the night waiting for daylight. With several GPSs we could assure the concerned rangers that we knew where we were going but with the

Hillsborough River rapids in Hillsborough River State Park.

obstructions it would be some time before we arrived at the takeout.

Our group of four continued down the river. We had a few wrong turns but managed to reach the boat ramp at John B. Sargent Park around 10:00 pm. Our staged car was farther down the river at the Morris Bridge Launch, so our only option was to walk back to Hillsborough State Park (about 11 miles). Happy to be off the river, we set off walking along US 301 trying to flag down any passing car. After about an hour or so of walking, a ranger pulled over and gave us a ride back to the campground. As we chatted about the adventure, I asked, "How many paddlers typically do this section of the river?" His answer was four! It was long after midnight by the time we happily settled into our tents.

Below 17 Runs, the middle section of the Hillsborough is a scenic, often canopied waterway that is popular with canoeists and kayakers with numerous launch sites and an outfitter that rents canoes and kayaks. Only an occasional snag can be present, depending on the water level.

The lower Hillsborough is where the river widens and is more suitable for motorboats. The culmination is a dramatic outflow into Hillsborough Bay where the river courses through downtown Tampa, a city of more than 400,000. Besides enjoying the river on the water, the city has built a paved riverwalk for great views from land. Tampa hosts a "Riverfest" on the riverwalk every year in late spring.

ALAFIA

Colorful people come and go along Florida's rivers, but perhaps the most unusual river residents were along the lower Alafia River near Tampa in the mid-twentieth century. The Giant's Fish Camp in Gibsonton sold mullet and other bait to catch tarpon for which the river was famous. It was run by Al Tomaini, the Giant of Alafia, listed as eight feet, four inches tall during his circus days. His fish camp assistants, many of them just over three feet tall, were either retired from the circus or taking a winter break.

Al's wife measured two feet, five inches because she was born without legs. Jeanie Tomaini had been billed

A paddler negotiates a small shoals area along the Alafia River.

quality issues in the past, mostly from phosphate mining, but the picturesque nature of the river, with its high banks and arching trees, is a major draw.

LITTLE MANATEE AND MANATEE

There is a lesson in Sun City. Envisioned as Florida's "Moving Picture City" in 1925, a large movie studio was built to attract Hollywood film producers, streets were named for the stars of the day, and lots were sold with the promise that people would be living with celebrities. A power plant and school were built, and utilities were buried. Florida was booming, so what could go wrong? When the Great Depression hit in the 1930s, Sun City was one of its first casualties. Boom-and-bust cycles are nothing new in Florida, and Sun City shows that development is not always the final blow to the natural world. When the world of man is abandoned, nature begins to take over again.

What survived Sun City intact is the Little Manatee River. Emerging from a swampy area near the former sawmill town of Fort Lonesome, the tannin-tinted waterway flows almost 40 miles along sandy banks before emptying into Tampa Bay. Like Sun City, Fort Lonesome is largely a ghost town. Its boom days came to an end when the steam-powered sawmill burned down.

The upper Little Manatee is narrow, twisty, and wild with a swift current and extensive canopy. A railroad bridge marks the location of the famous "Orange Blossom Special" train that was immortalized by a fast-moving fiddle tune of the same name, written by Ervin T. Rouse in 1938. The tune, played by both famous and aspiring fiddle players throughout North America, is often referred to as the fiddle player's national anthem.

About four and a half miles of the middle section of river flows through Little Manatee River State Park where the stream can also be viewed from several nature trails. The lower Little Manatee, popular with boaters, widens and fans out into a tidal marsh just north of Cockroach Bay. Given the name, do manatees actually use the river? The gentle giants are often seen munching on shoreline vegetation in the summer months. The same is true for the nearby Manatee River, which begins at the Lake Manatee Dam and flows into Tampa Bay. This river widens considerably after only six miles, making the lower portion more suitable for motorboats.

The upper Manatee River harkens back to the area's pioneer history because the Rye Preserve contains the

Al Tomaini in the 1940s with friends.
HENNEPIN COUNTY LIBRARY, MINNESOTA

as the Living Half Girl, and together, the circus billed them as the World's Strangest Married Couple. But on the Alafia River, they were just people who loved the river and were popular among anglers. "A finer fellow you'd never see," wrote Rube Allyn in 1957. Al Tomaini died of a pituitary tumor in 1962 at age 50, but Jeanie lived until 1999.

The lower Alafia River is still known for its fishing, although the upper river is primarily frequented by paddlers since there are often shoals and ledges to negotiate. Several miles of shoreline are publicly owned and maintained by Hillsborough County or the Florida Park Service. Two popular spots along the river are Lithia Springs Conservation Park and Alafia River State Park. The 26-mile river has been plagued by water

If ever a river is "different," it's the Little Manatee, so different in fact that some years ago, Hollywood movie makers "discovered" this amazing stream—and forthwith set up shop on her banks. Combines, unions and red tape, joined in a successful effort to keep Florida out of the movie business, so the City of "Sun City," once planned as Florida's cinema capital, today rests peacefully mouldering on her picturesque banks.

—RUBE ALLYN, *OUTDOORS AFLOAT*, 1957

The Little Manatee River.

last remaining remnant of the old Rye river community, the Rye Family Cemetery. The river's shoreline was also the site of Fort Hamer, built to defend area settlers during skirmishes with Seminole Indians in 1849. No trace of the fort exists today.

MYAKKA

It is no surprise the Myakka River was Florida's first state-designated wild and scenic river in 1985. Most of the river flows through protected conservation lands, including one of the largest state parks in the system, the 37,000-acre Myakka River State Park. The efforts began in 1934 when a newly formed sportsman's club lobbied for wildlife protection laws and the establishment of a Civilian Conservation Corps camp along the banks of the Myakka River. The workers in this Depression-era program then built one of Florida's first state parks, one that included log cabins, a campground, trails, and boat launches, not to mention the roads and bridges for vehicle access. As a result of careful protection, the park has become known for its wildlife—panther, turkey, sandhill cranes, bald eagles, scores of colorful wading and migratory birds, and alligators—thousands and thousands of alligators.

Alligators are abundant in all parts of the river and in the park's upper and lower lakes that the river runs through. In fact, the alligators move depending

An alligator walking along the Myakka River. The river is known for its large and numerous gators.

What's so special about the Myakka? Why do young couples choose Myakka for their weddings? Why do families scattered across the country make pilgrimages back for reunions year after year? Why do some choose to spend all eternity here, their ashes discreetly spread along the banks of the river by family and friends? And why is it that "old-timers" sojourn back to see this special place one more time or decide to invest the last leisurely days of their lives here, pursuing activities they always dreamed of having time for?

—P. J. BENSHOFF, *MYAKKA*

Bird life, including black-necked stilts, is also abundant along the Myakka River.

on water levels and food sources. They are especially abundant in the remote 7,500-acre wilderness area of the park at the "deep hole," part of the lower lake. The deep hole is actually a 200-foot-wide sinkhole that is around 130 to 140 feet deep, but divers are wary about venturing into its depths for an exact measurement. At times, a couple of hundred alligators congregate around the deep hole, likely because they can be assured of deep water in all conditions, and it's also a place where fish and wading birds can be plentiful. Humans are not abundant in the wilderness preserve, however. They are limited to 30 per day and that includes both hikers and paddlers on the river.

The bulk of park visitors congregate around the park's upper lake where large tour boats motor around the lake, allowing visitors to view alligators from a safe distance. Wild pigs are often seen as well, a nuisance animal first brought by the Spanish. Wild pigs turn shorelines and river floodplains into what appear to be freshly plowed farm fields as they search for grubs, so the park licenses hunters to dispatch them. Alligators take their share as well.

Another highlight in the park is the canopy walkway suspended 25 feet above the ground and anchored by a tall tower that soars 74 feet. The summit allows for a spectacular view of the Myakka floodplain and adjoining hammock forests dominated by live oaks and sabal palm trees. The walkway and tower were built and maintained by an active group of park volunteers. The waterways and lush green forests that can be seen in all directions are a testament to the foresight of a small group of sportsmen many decades ago.

FISHEATING CREEK

Renowned black-and-white landscape photographer Clyde Butcher credits Fisheating Creek and its tributaries with opening his eyes to the beauty of interior South Florida, and it's no wonder. Billowy clouds often float over a wild, cypress-lined stream in a scene reminiscent of "Highwaymen" paintings. Alligators sun along swampy shores while stark white egrets and ibis seem to glow against dark water.

Fisheating Creek is the wildest of Lake Okeechobee's feeder streams, emerging from swamps 52 miles upstream and flowing through the Fisheating Creek Wildlife Management Area. Its water is clean. Its shores are unmarred by development. It is a wildlife haven and fishermen's paradise.

Several years ago, I explored the river with a local guide, Bill Clement. He had been coming to Fisheating Creek for most of his life, that is, except for a 10-year period between 1989 and 1999 when river access was blocked by private landowners, the Lykes Brothers Corporation. Now the shores of Fisheating Creek are either public property or open to public access, and Clement was under contract with the FWC to keep the river clean and to clear enough of the channel to make it navigable for boats, canoes, and kayaks.

"It's not easy," he says. "The river is always changing. It rises and falls. Trees fall into it. Banks erode. But sometimes I have to pinch myself to remind me that I'm working. Occasionally, I cut off the engine and just drift and listen to the sounds of nature."

As Clement motored me up and down the river, that overused and often misused phrase to describe Florida kept popping into my head—"paradise." The river has miraculously survived in a region where most rivers and streams have been channelized, heavily polluted by cattle and agricultural runoff, or lined with fish camps and vacation homes.

Around every bend, it seemed, there were herons and egrets, wood storks and ibis. Alligators plunged into the water as we passed, one after the other, like crocodiles chasing Johnny Weismuller in an old Tarzan flick. "There's no shortage of gators," announced Clement. Some of the monsters appeared to be 10 feet or more in length, but I didn't jump out to measure. I was mindful that an archery hunter was once attacked by a hefty gator as he tried to swim across the creek. The hunter survived; the gator was quickly dispatched by FWC officers.

The river alternated from being narrow and twisted, with many divergent channels, to being open and wide. The wide areas have been labeled "lakes." Clement called out their names as we passed through: "Rock Lake, Picnic Lake, Lemon Lake. . . ." Many spots have local lore and history attached to them, such as the memorial cypress where young people swim. The ashes of one popular resident were spread at the foot of the tree after he died while helping with an auto accident that occurred on nearby Highway 27.

Several local couples have been married at Fisheating Creek, and many of those same couples renew their

The Thlo-thlo-pop-ka, or Fish-Eating Creek, runs through an open prairie, to which it serves as a drain. As might be expected, it gives evidence of being in the wet season a large stream, but when I examined it the volume of water it discharged was very small. This stream is very tortuous, and sometimes swells into a river, and then dwindles into a brook. Its head is in a marshy prairie, where a number of streamlets run together about twenty miles in a straight line, due east to the Oke-chobee, but following the course of the creek about twice that distance. The banks of Fish-Eating Creek are covered with game, and its waters filled with fish.

—LIEUTENANT JOHN RODGERS, 1842

After hauling the canoes over two troublesome places re-entered the creek, a beautiful stream, clear, with a beautiful white sandy bottom. Pulled against the current to the Sd & Wd. Saw immense flocks of cranes, pink spoonbills, curlew, and wild turkeys in plenty. Also, a large number of alligators killed; killed two small ones and cut off their tails for eating; caught a soft-shelled and a hard-shelled turtle and had them cooked for supper, with a fry of some little fish that foolishly jumped into one of the canoes. Our camping-ground the prettiest by far that we have had. Two veteran cypress stretched their scraggy arms over our camp, draped in moss to the very ground. The day was rendered harmonious by the warblings of multitudes of feathered choristers, and the night hideous with the splash of alligators, hooting of owls, and screamings of a variety of unquiet night-birds.

—GEORGE HENRY PREBLE, 1842

vows along the creek's wild shores. The stream has interwoven itself into the lives of many.

Before the 10-year legal battle that swirled around river access, the Lykes Brothers ran a large camping and canoe business near the Highway 27 Bridge. That business has now been reopened by a private entrepreneur through a contract with the FWC. While emotions ran high during the legal battle, most are pleased with the outcome. The entire river is public property and open for public use. The Lykes Corporation received a fair price and retained ownership to some of its river lands while selling its development rights to the state. The river is clean, there is little trash, and there is a more visible law enforcement presence. Clement credits the Lykes Corporation for helping to protect the river during its stewardship. "They could have cut all the trees and built houses," he said.

According to then campground concessionaire and conservationist, Ellen Peterson, there is something about the creek that draws people. "It's probably the most magical place in Florida," said Peterson.

Peterson formed a "memory book" of photos and stories from generations of people who have fond recollections of growing up near the creek, of hunting, fishing, courtships, baptisms, and marriages. "I recently had an old-timer's potluck here where we ate and told lies around a campfire of how it used to be," she said. She also noted that astronomy groups often visit the creek because it is one of the few places in Southwest Florida unmarred by artificial lights.

Wildlife watchers come to Fisheating Creek to view alligators, wading birds, and otters, always hoping for that rare glimpse of a Florida panther or black bear, two species that frequent the area. In summer, there's a good chance of spotting swallow-tailed kites, which feed on insects along the creek. They are highly social and often hunt in large groups, a rare trait for a bird of prey.

At the base of the creek, near where it meets Lake Okeechobee, the largest swallow-tailed kite rookery in North America boasts an estimated 3,000 birds during the peak roosting season of late July, representing about 60 percent of the total North American population.

"I cannot overstate the importance of this site," said Dr. Ken Meyer of the Avian Research and Conservation Center in Gainesville. Under contract with the FWC, Meyer has intensively studied

Fisheating Creek is known for its wild scenery.

As far as the eye can see at times, there is a vast sea of vivid green rolling onward toward the horizon. The banks are lined with small trees and shrubs, which in spring burst into flowers and new foliage, and it is a very paradise of gorgeous, if unmusical, birds that fill the air with their croaking and screaming.

—NEVIN O. WINTER, *FLORIDA, THE LAND OF ENCHANTMENT,* 1918

the kites for several years. "We have evidence that they gain 20 to 25 percent of their body weight within a few weeks during this time of year [summer] as they prepare to migrate."

According to Meyer, the roosting kites are extremely sensitive to disturbances. A few years ago, they moved from their historic roost of native cypress trees to some Australian pines, possibly due to airboats. Meyer is trying to lure the birds back to their historic roost by using kite decoys in the trees. To minimize human disturbance, the FWC has adopted a one-mile buffer around both the current and historic roosting sites from late June through early September.

Meyer claims the historic site offers several advantages for the birds and for wildlife managers. It is possible to control human access, and a wildlife viewing blind could be built a safe distance away. "We want people to see this," he said. "It's very educational; it's very inspiring, but it's also very important that we do not disturb these birds. They're not just there to hang out. They're preparing for a very arduous 5,000-mile journey to southern Brazil and eastern Paraguay. Storing energy is very important to them and expending energy can be costly."

Like the kites, Ellen Peterson noticed certain people coming back to the creek year after year. "People even bring their babies with them and tell me they want them to see what natural Florida is like," she said. "Once you come to Fisheating Creek, you always come back."

KISSIMMEE

Seminole Indians once plied the waters of the Kissimmee River and Kissimmee chain of lakes. They camped on wild islands and shorelines, fished the waters, encountered numerous alligators, and reveled in soaring bald eagles, ospreys, and snail kites. Similar sights and adventures can be experienced today in the Everglades headwaters between Orlando and Lake Okeechobee.

In the spirit of those early Seminoles, I joined a 12-day, 140-mile kayaking and hiking expedition in the spring of 2007. Consisting of volunteer outdoors people and government employees, the expedition sought to showcase restoration efforts of the Kissimmee River and Kissimmee chain of lakes and to investigate the potential for developing a public paddling and hiking trail, complementing the existing Florida Trail footpath along the Kissimmee River. I represented the

A Fisheating Creek cypress stand.

The river's origin is Shingle Creek, a surprisingly wild waterway near Orlando.

Florida Department of Environmental Protection's Office of Greenways and Trails.

The driving force behind the idea was Harris Rosen, an Orlando resort developer whose newest resort was along Shingle Creek, considered the headwaters of the Everglades. "When I purchased the land," said the former hotel planner for Walt Disney, "I didn't realize Shingle Creek even existed until I flew over the property in a helicopter." Rosen helped to line up key government and private sponsors for the expedition, along with a documentary crew from Bright House Networks.

For the next several days, we experienced a Florida few ever know, from old-style fish camps and cattle ranches to a restored river with abundant alligators, bird life, and expansive views of marshy expanses, broken only by tree islands covered in live oaks. Many believed it was the first time anyone had paddled this span of water in its entirety since the Seminole Indians more than a century before.

Like our 12-day journey, the Kissimmee River has been on an incredible journey for more than a century. The river's origin is cypress-lined Shingle Creek just south of Orlando, a place where early settlers cut the centuries-old cypress for shingles and other uses, thus the name "Shingle Creek." Remnants of those early structures can still be found, and others may be moved to the new park from the nearby Pioneer Village.

Near the present-day Kissimmee Airport, during the Second Seminole War, Coacoochee—also known as Wild Cat—and his warriors were engaged in a running battle with General Thomas Jesup and a thousand troops when they retreated into the thick cypress swamps around Shingle Creek. The soldiers turned back at that point. Swamps were an impediment to a large army, and a great advantage for stealthy Seminoles. And now this swamp had become a modern refuge in the heart of an urban area.

Shingle Creek spills out into Lake Tohopekaliga, one of several large connected lakes. In this massive lake is the 132-acre Makinson Island. Once slated for a resort hotel and timeshare development and now publicly owned, Makinson Island is a magical place with nesting bald eagles and swooping snail kites. This is where Wild Cat was born around 1807. Perhaps his presence and that of his people still inhabit the large island. Some suggest the Seminole name for the island was the same as the lake—Tohopekaliga, or "fortress place." Thick trees provided the

The Kissimmee is a deep, rapid stream, generally running through a marshy plain, but sometimes the pine land approaches its borders, and sometimes beautiful live-oak hummocks fringe its banks. The In-to-keetah, or Deer-Driving Place, is a pretty little lake, with an island of perhaps one hundred acres of very fine land. "There," said the guide, "the Indians once lived in very great numbers, and many may yet remain"; so our boats were concealed, and we waited for night to make an examination, when the fires would point out the exact position of any party; but though appearances proved the first part of our guide's assertion, we found the town had long been deserted.

—LIEUTENANT JOHN RODGERS, 1842

Seminoles with cover, and since canoes were kept on opposite ends of the island, escape was always possible.

Other lakes in the Kissimmee chain include Cypress, Hatchineha, and Kissimmee. Long ago, the Kissimmee River connected the lakes, with passage suitable for dugout canoes. But nineteenth-century steamships were a different matter, so canals were dredged between the lakes and, eventually, locks were built for flood control. The canals had a dual purpose, as they also drained adjacent swamps and floodplains so more land could be used for ranching. In the past few years, the South Florida Water Management District has purchased vast tracts of former floodplain along the entire watershed—more than 100,000 acres in all—so that the chain of lakes and the Kissimmee River can once again

pulse with the ebb and flow of wet and dry seasons. The state of Florida also has been buying additional tracts for recreation and wildlife protection.

The lakes feature old Florida-style fish camps such as Camp Mack, where fishermen and hunters sit around a smoldering fire in front of the camp store day and night. Amusing restroom door signs greet guests—either "Inboard" or "Outboard."

Along the undeveloped shoreline of the massive Lake Kissimmee, a line of marsh, pickerelweed, duck potato, and lily pads help to buffer any waves. Midges, small mosquito-shaped insects that swarm but don't bite, can be prevalent in spring. Locals call them "chizzy winks." You have to be careful when opening your mouth or you can ingest extra protein. Also in the

Hotel Kissimmee on the shores of Lake Tohopekaliga, from Scenes in Florida. W. W. WRENN, SAVANNAH, GEORGIA

Horses wade in the old channel of the Kissimmee River between Lake Cypress and Lake Hatchineha.

marshes are fishermen in boats who gather in clusters to fish for bream and bass.

In the midst of Lake Kissimmee is Brahma Island. At 4,000 acres, Brahma Island is famous for its large wild boars and bald eagles, claiming the largest concentration of nonmigratory bald eagles in the lower 48 states. Eagles are everywhere—in trees, circling in the sky, or swooping over the lake or dry prairies. An estimated 80 to100 eagles live on the island. In the early 1800s, Seminole chief Alligator and his band once lived on the island before being driven out by Zachary Taylor and his forces during the Second Seminole War.

Cary Lightsey, co-owner with his brother of Brahma Island, is a sixth-generation Florida cattle rancher. He and his family sold much of their development rights to the state so that future generations of Lightseys can maintain the family business and not sell the land for housing. His family has always had a philosophy of leaving at least 40 percent of their land native. "Florida has a very sensitive ecosystem," he said. "And I'm afraid if we go in there and start rearranging God's creation it might come back to bite you someday."

At the S-65 Lock, the Kissimmee River begins just south of Lake Kissimmee as the C-38 Canal. Bordering

The wide and marshy Kissimmee River floodplain alongside the Florida Trail.

this arrow-straight canal are tall angular spoil piles created by the canal dredging, appearing much like modern effigy mounds from an engineer's dream world.

The Kissimmee was once a 103-mile natural waterway. From 1962 through 1971, the U.S. Army Corps of Engineers cut a straight ditch through the river's heart, hoping to better control flooding in the upper system. As a result, fish, waterfowl, and other wildlife drastically declined and water was no longer being filtered by a slow meandering river channel through thousands of acres of marshlands. Lake Okeechobee received too much water too quickly during the rainy season, and the water quality was severely degraded.

Fortunately, in 1999, restoration of the Kissimmee River began—a truly momentous occasion. Huge dump trucks began carrying dirt from former spoil piles to fill sections of canal while water was diverted to restore the old winding river channel. A key dam on the river was blown up, and more than 40 miles of the original Kissimmee River was restored.

Almost immediately along the restored river, the return of seasonal sheet flow began to heal the ecosystem. Alligators rose in abundance along with bird life—limpkins, green herons, yellow-legs, stilts, cormorants, and many others. Since the restoration, biologists have observed several species of shorebirds that had not been seen in several decades, and they also documented the return of migratory fowl and an increased fishery. The Kissimmee, at least the middle segment, was back!

In places, the winding Kissimmee resembles a river through a prairie, its marshy floodplain at least two miles wide, vast, and windswept. "It feels like we're in Kansas or Nebraska," kayaker Julia Recker observed on the 2007 expedition. "Seeing this, and you realize why the channelization of the Kissimmee River was a crime against nature."

The restored Kissimmee River is now a paddling trail and a boon to anglers and birdwatchers. Already, primitive campsites have been set up by the South Florida Water Management District for those seeking overnight adventures. And some may want to begin their journey at Shingle Creek and travel the entire chain of lakes and river to Lake Okeechobee, following the path of Seminole Indians more than a century ago.

LOXAHATCHEE

The Loxahatchee was not designated Florida's first national wild and scenic river in 1985 for being lined with houses. The winding yellow-black water traverses one of Southeast Florida's wildest domains: the 11,500-acre Jonathan Dickinson State Park.

The upper river is closed to motorboats, so canoeists and kayakers launch from Palm Beach County's scenic River Bend Park. Only these smaller craft could navigate the narrow twists and turns of the river anyway. Paddlers are soon immersed beneath a canopy of old-growth cypress trees mixed with arching palms. Leathery ferns tower over watercraft. Crying kingfishers dart in and out of openings, and the raps of woodpeckers and occasional squawks of herons pierce the air.

Around most bends, turtles sun themselves on logs, their legs splayed out to help them cool their bodies. These are the creatures that inspired Seminole Indians to give the river its name, although the proper Seminole name was Loh-juh Hatchee, or "turtle river." The pronunciation of many Seminole place names have been corrupted over time. But with regard to the Loxahatchee, the Seminoles could also have named it the Hul-bah-duh Hatchee—"alligator river." On more than one narrow bend, the sunning beasts will match an average kayak in length and girth.

According to the late Seminole leader Betty Mae Jumper, in her autobiography *A Seminole Legend*, the Loxahatchee River did bear a different name at one time. During the Second Seminole War, Jumper's ancestors were camped on the Loxahatchee River

The vegetation is so thick and the scene so wild that it seems we are on the Congo instead of the Loxahatchee.

—HAROLD C. ROLLS, *PALM BEACH POST,* 1923

Above: Young alligators along the Loxahatchee River.
Facing page: Vertical view of paddling the Loxahatchee River.

thinking that a peace agreement was still in place—The Macomb Treaty. "One day when most of the men were out hunting, soldiers suddenly came and surrounded a camp of Seminoles, mostly old men, women, and children, along a river," she wrote. "That is why the river there from that day on was called 'Lo-tsa-hatchee,' meaning 'River of Lies' in Creek, because our people thought that peace had been made. The soldiers gathered the Indians like criminals, making them all sit down in the open fields. Some were lucky enough to run away, and those who escaped ran to other camps to warn them." The name Lo-tsa-hatchee was later changed to Loxahatchee, "river of turtles."

The last major battle of the Second Seminole War also occurred along the shores of the swampy stream. Major General Thomas Jesup encountered a group of Seminoles in late January 1838. A fierce battle was fought as Seminole warriors held off Jesup's superior force long enough for their families to retreat. Then, as in so many other Seminole war battles, the warriors stealthily vanished into the vast swamps.

Fortunately, the Loxahatchee is peaceful now, only battered by the occasional hurricane. Two small log dams or weirs require portaging. You can hear the falling water long before reaching the structures. The dams were originally constructed in the 1930s by local families to maintain water levels for farm irrigation, and they are maintained primarily for historical purposes. Being rather rustic in appearance, they seem to fit in with the river's wild nature. Plus, they help keep water levels high enough for paddling. Wood drag-over ramps make for easy portaging around the dams.

Despite man's best efforts, nature can still block the Loxahatchee channel. In 2004 and 2005, three hurricanes effectively closed the river to paddlers for almost six months until crews could clear a path. During dry months, usually from February to early summer, some portaging in the river channel is generally necessary due to low water.

Roughly the midpoint on the paddling trail is Trapper Nelson's Homestead, a state park interpretive site. This also marks the point where the Loxahatchee widens and becomes a mangrove-lined estuary. Tides exert a strong influence.

Cypress boardwalk at Trapper Nelson's on the Loxahatchee River.

Loxahatchee River reflections.

Trapper Nelson, known as the "Wild Man of the Loxahatchee," settled the area in the 1930s and remained until his death in 1968. He made a living by trapping animals for pelts, selling animals to zoos and visitors, selling firewood, playing poker with visitors, and caging live critters in pens for paying customers. His concrete snake pit of live rattlesnakes was highly popular.

Trapper—muscular and tanned—would usually greet visitors shirtless, a hefty indigo snake draped over his neck. Shorts and a pith helmet completed the outfit. Trapper was quick with a smile and tall tale, and he loved to mooch food off of visitors. Tourists, celebrities, local residents, and school kids all beat a path to the legendary homestead. They paid an entrance fee of 50 cents for adults and 25 cents for children. People could also rent one of the rustic guest cabins and freely use the stout rope swing over the river. "It may be hard for some people today to envision, but back then, to all these northerners, the Loxahatchee was just as exciting as going up the Amazon," said Nathaniel Reed in *Life and Death on the Loxahatchee: The Story of Trapper Nelson*, by James Snyder. "You expected to see Tarzan just around the corner—only in this case, there he was!"

Trapper did use banks, especially since he bought and sold land along the river, but the park service found a hidden cache of silver coins several years after they acquired the site, most likely from entrance fees to his zoo.

To tour the trapper's homestead is to tour a piece of Old Florida, harkening back to an era not that long ago when most of Florida was wild and land was relatively cheap. The cabins and outbuildings, along with the dock and boardwalk, have all been hewn by hand, primarily built out of old-growth cypress and pine. The Florida Park Service maintains the original appearance as best it can, and it seems to be the perfect human complement to the wild Loxahatchee, river of turtles.

Other popular paddling trails in the region include the north and south forks of the St. Lucie River, with the south fork having a more wilderness nature.

MIAMI

Tequesta Indians, and later Seminoles, once canoed the Miami River. The river formerly drained part of the eastern Everglades, with rapids on its two main forks. It is now a highly altered but fascinating urban river of five and a half miles. Vessels of nearly all types, from sailboats to freighters, now use the waterway, and the lower river is a major seaport. A point of interest is the Miami Circle, built by the Tequesta people 1,700 to 2,000 years ago at the mouth of the Miami River. Discovered in 1998 during clearing for a condominium, the circle is 38 feet in diameter and consists of 24 holes. Shell tools, stone axes, and other artifacts were found at the site along with the remains of a shark, dolphin, and sea turtle. It was likely a ceremonial site and is now preserved as a park.

Just at the border of the garden of the Royal Palm Hotel the Miami River empties into Bay Biscayne. This stream meanders through the whole town, and is lined with picturesque quays and wharves, alongside which white yachts and little sailing boats are moored. In the early morning, with the sun's rays slanting across the lines of the wharves, and the mist just rising from the river, this is a very beautiful scene.

—JOHN MARTIN HAMMOND, *WINTER JOURNEYS IN THE SOUTH,* 1916

Seminole Indians paddling the Miami River, circa 1915. J. N. CHAMBERLAIN, MIAMI, FLORIDA

HELPING OUR RIVERS

4

Clean water protest at the Florida Department of Environmental Protection, July 26, 2016.

157

If we are all students in this great shared learning process of life, then perhaps we can see the river as a great lesson in ecology, as a metaphor for learning how the integration of each natural part affects the whole.

—BILL BELLEVILLE, *RIVER OF LAKES*

We never know the worth of water till the well is dry.

—THOMAS FULLER, *GNOMOLOGIA*, 1732

There is sufficiency in the world for man's need but not for man's greed.

—MOHANDAS K. GANDHI

The more clearly we can focus our attention on the wonders and realities of the universe about us, the less taste we shall have for destruction.

—RACHEL CARSON

People who live along or frequently visit a river often develop a personal relationship that is familial. But instead of thinking of the river as a child growing up or as an elder eventually passing from this earthly existence, the river spans innumerable generations. It is more like a living ancestor that will transcend any lifetime. We simply experience it for just a short time in the geologic sense. Perhaps that is part of the attraction. In some ways, we are no different than the current generation of fish, birds, alligators, manatees, and otters that frequent a river, the main difference being that our species has the power to destroy. That is why we need river advocates.

In 1966, the Hudson River Fishermen's Association (now Hudson Riverkeeper) was formed to address massive industrial pollution along the Hudson River. Robert F. Kennedy Jr. became its chief prosecuting attorney in 1984, adding a brighter spotlight to the movement. The group's success eventually spawned similar groups, and in 1999, the Waterkeeper Alliance was established as an umbrella organization for more than 350 Waterkeeper organizations and affiliates on six continents. In Florida, more than a dozen Riverkeeper groups are allied through Waterkeepers Florida. These groups usually consist of a small paid staff and a "riverkeeper" to advocate for river protection and restoration, although some are completely run by volunteers.

Another national river group, the American Rivers Conservation Council (now American Rivers) was established in 1973 to fight unnecessary damming of the country's last wild and scenic rivers.

Springs protection is also central to healthy Florida rivers. One group, the Howard T. Odom Florida Springs Institute, focuses on restoring and protecting springs throughout the state. The group's executive director, Bob Knight, advocates for steps that include restoring spring flows to levels that protect their ecological health by placing a protective cap on groundwater pumping and charging a fee for groundwater withdrawals, restoring springs and aquifer water quality by regulating all fertilizer use in Florida and charging a fee for use, and reducing the use of septic tanks to treat human waste.

The idea these groups uphold is that every river system, including their associated springs, needs a champion or champions because rivers cannot lobby or vote, they cannot write letters or sign petitions, and they cannot sue in court. They can only inspire. And so it is up to us.

A recent trend is for rivers to be provided the same legal rights as humans. It began in 2017 in New Zealand when the Maori *iwi* (tribe) won a 140-year legal battle to recognize the Whanganui River as an ancestor with legal status as a living entity. The idea is to treat the river as an "indivisible whole, instead of the traditional model for the last 100 years of treating it from a perspective of ownership and management," said lead *iwi* negotiator Gerrard Albert, quoted by Michael Safi in *The Guardian* that year. This was followed by a similar ruling for India's Ganges and its main tributary, the Yamuna. The Ganges is considered sacred by more than 1 billion Indians, but it has suffered from massive

A kayaker carrying a rusty barrel picked up along the Weeki Wachee River.

pollution. However, the ruling was overruled by a higher court since a practical way to implement legal protections was unclear.

Also in 2017, the Constitutional Court in Columbia granted legal personhood to the Rio Atrato, a river that flows through the territories of 91 different indigenous communities. Fourteen legal guardians from communities impacted by mining and pollution were appointed to an Atrato Guardians Commission. It was considered a good first step in protecting and restoring the river and changing our viewpoint from being in the center of nature—in control—to being part of the whole.

In Florida, the 2020 Florida Legislature outlawed the granting of legal rights to rivers in an attempt to thwart initial moves to grant personhood rights to the Santa Fe and other rivers. That doesn't prevent people from placing rivers in higher regard, however, and pushing for greater protections.

BIBLIOGRAPHY

Alberson, Sarah D. "King of the Crackers." *Florida Wildlife*, June 1953.

Allyn, Rube. *Outdoors Afloat*. St. Petersburg, FL: Great Outdoors Publishing, 1957.

Barbour, George M. *Florida for Tourists, Invalids, and Settlers*. New York, D. Appleton and Company, 1882.

Bartram, William. *Travels through North and South Carolina, Georgia, East and West Florida*. Philadelphia: James and Johnson, 1791; Dover Edition, 1955.

Belleville, Bill. *River of Lakes: A Journey on Florida's St. Johns River*. Athens and London: University of Georgia Press, 2000.

Benshoff, P. J. *Myakka*. Sarasota, FL: Pineapple Press, 2002.

Boning, Charles R. *Florida's Rivers*, 2nd ed. Sarasota, FL: Pineapple Press, 2016.

Brown, Canter, Jr. *Florida's Peace River Frontier*. Orlando: University of Central Florida Press, 1991.

Burt, Al. *Al Burt's Florida: Snowbirds, Sand Castles, and Self-Rising Crackers*. Gainesville: University Press of Florida, 1997.

Cabell, Branch, and A. J. Hanna. *The St. Johns: A Parade of Diversities*. New York and Toronto: Farrar & Rinehart, 1943.

Callaway, E. E. *In the Beginning*. Dayton, OH: ITB Associates, 1971.

Carr, Archie. *A Naturalist in Florida: A Celebration of Eden*. New Haven, CT, and London: Yale University Press, 1994.

Cerulean, Susan, Janisse Ray, and Laura Newton. *Between Two Rivers: Stories from the Red Hills to the Gulf*. Tallahassee, FL: Red Hills Writers Project, 2004.

Deland, Margaret. *Florida Days*. Boston: Little, Brown and Company, 1889.

Dimock, A. W. *Florida Enchantments*. New York: Frederick A. Stokes Company, 1926.

Hammond, John Martin. *Winter Journeys in the South*. Philadelphia and London: J. B. Lippincott Company, 1916.

Hill, Beverly. "Kayaking at Morrison Springs in Walton County, Florida." Northwest Florida Outdoor Adventure, July 10, 2011. http://www.northwestfloridaoutdooradventure.com/2011/07/10/kayaking-at-morrison-springs-in-walton-county-florida/.

Hill, Geoffrey. *Ivorybill Hunters: The Search for Proof in a Flooded Wilderness*. New York: Oxford University Press, 2007.

Jahoda, Gloria. *River of the Golden Ibis*. Gainesville: University Press of Florida, 2000.

Jumper, Betty Mae Tiger, and Patsy West, *A Seminole Legend: The Life of Betty Mae Tiger Jumper*. Gainesville: University Press of Florida, 2001.

Key, Alexander. *The Wrath and the Wind*. New York: Bobbs-Merrill, 1949.

Klinkenberg, Jeff. "The Wild Man of Lily Spring." *Tampa Bay Times*, Sept. 27, 2005.

Knight, Robert L. "A New Year's Resolution for Florida's Springs." *Citrus County Chronicle*, January 17, 2020.

———. *Silenced Springs: Moving from Tragedy to Hope*. Gainesville: Howard T. Odom Florida Springs Institute, 2015.

Lanier, Sidney. *Florida: Its Scenery, Climate, and History*. Philadelphia: J. B. Lippincott & Co., 1876.

Laumer, Frank (ed.). *Amidst a Storm of Bullets: The Diary of Lt. Henry Prince in Florida 1836–1842*. Tampa, FL: University of Tampa Press, 1998.

Lenz, Richard J. "Ochlockonee River." Tallahassee, FL: Tall Timbers Research Station, n.d.

Leonard, Irving A. (ed.). "A Lost 'Psyche': Kirk Munroe's Log of a 1,600 Mile Canoe Cruise in Florida Waters, 1881–1882." *Tequesta*, no. 27, 1968.

Mahon, John. *History of the Second Seminole War 1835–1842*, rev. ed. Gainesville: University Press of Florida, 1985.

Marth, Del, and Marty Marth. *The Rivers of Florida*. Sarasota, FL: Pineapple Press, 1990.

Matschat, Cecile Hulse. *Suwannee River: Strange Green Land*. New York: Farrar and Rinehart, 1938.

"Miami Circle National Historic Landmark." Trails of Florida's Indian Heritage. Accessed February 29, 2020. https://www.trailoffloridasindianheritage.org/miami-circle.

Missal, John, and Mary Lou Missall. *The Seminole Wars*. Gainesville: University Press of Florida, 2004.

Motte, J. R. *Journey into Wilderness*. Gainesville: University Press of Florida, 1963.

Nixon, Richard. "Statement about Halting Construction of the Cross Florida Barge Canal." American Presidency Project. Accessed September 2, 2018. http://www.presidency.ucsb.edu/ws/index.php?pid=3044.

Nox, Owen. *Southern Rambles: Florida*. Boston: A. Williams & Company, 1881.

"Okefenokee Swamp and St. Marys River named among America's Most Endangered Rivers of 2020." Staff report, *Savannah Business Journal*, April 14, 2020.

Owens, Harry P. *Apalachicola before 1861*. Tallahassee, FL: Sentry Press, 2014.

Packard, Winthrop. *Florida Trails*. Boston: Small, Maynard and Company, 1910.

"Peace River Natural History." Southwest Florida Water Management District. Accessed July 22, 2016. http://www.swfwmd.state.fl.us/education/interactive/peaceriver/natural.php.

"Perdido River Water Management Area." Northwest Florida Water Management District. Accessed February 22, 2020. https://www.nwfwater.com/Lands/Recreation/Area/Perdido-River.

Preble, George Henry. "A Canoe Expedition into the Everglades in 1842." *Tequesta*, no. 5, 1945.

"The River Ecology." St. Johns Riverkeeper. Accessed February 3, 2019. http://www.stjohnsriverkeeper.org/the-river/ecology/.

"Riverkeeper Timeline." Riverkeeper. Accessed January 20, 2020. https://www.riverkeeper.org/riverkeeper-mission/our-story/timeline/.

Rogers, G. M. "The Ochlockonee: Yesterday and Today." *Florida Wildlife*, March–April 1994.

Safi, Michael. "Ganges and Yamuna Rivers Granted Same Legal Rights as Human Beings." *The Guardian*, March 21, 2017. https://www.theguardian.com/world/2017/mar/21/ganges-and-yamuna-rivers-granted-same-legal-rights-as-human-beings.

"The St. Johns River–Fast Facts." St. Johns River Water Management District. Accessed January 30, 2020. https://nbbd.com/godo/StJohns.html.

"St. Marys River." Georgia River Network. Accessed February 27, 2020. https://garivers.org/st-marys-river/.

"Silver Springs." Florida Springs Institute. Accessed December 26, 2018. http://www.floridasprings.org/protecting/featured/silver%20springs/.

Snyder, James D. *Life and Death on the Loxahatchee: The Story of Trapper Nelson*, new rev. ed. Jupiter, FL: Pharos Books, 2004.

Spear, Kevin. "Does Bar Hurt Wekiva River or Let More Appreciate It?" *Orlando Sentinel*, September 4, 2010. http://www.orlandosentinel.com/business/tourism/os-wekiva-party-place-controversy-20100903,0,5566059.story.

Stamm, Doug. *The Springs of Florida*, 2nd ed. Sarasota, FL: Pineapple Press, 2008.

"The Strangest Couple in the World: Al and Jeannie Tomaini." International Independent Showmen's Museum. Accessed January 19, 2020. https://showmensmuseum.org/exhibits/strangest-couple-world/.

"Sun City." Ghost Towns. Accessed February 23, 2020. https://www.ghosttowns.com/states/fl/suncity.html.

Vickers, Lu, and Sara Dione. *Weeki Wachee: City of Mermaids*. Gainesville: University Press of Florida, 2007.

Watts, Betty M. *The Watery Wilderness of Apalach, Florida*. Tallahassee, FL: Apalach Books, 1975.

Winter, Nevin O. *Florida, The Land of Enchantment*. Boston: The Page Company, 1918.

Works Progress Administration. *Florida: A Guide to the Southernmost State*. New York: Oxford University Press, 1939.

INDEX

ABOUT THE AUTHOR

Doug Alderson is the author of several books, including *America's Alligator*, *Wild Florida Waters*, *Waters Less Traveled*, *New Dawn for the Kissimmee River*, *Encounters with Florida's Endangered Wildlife*, and *A New Guide to Old Florida Attractions*, which the Florida Writers Association placed in the top five published books for 2017. He has won four first-place Royal Palm Literary awards for travel books, and several other state and national writing and photography awards. Additionally, his articles and photographs have been featured in magazines such as *Sea Kayaker*, *Coast and Kayak*, *Wildlife Conservation*, *Native Peoples*, *American Forests*, *Sierra*, *Mother Earth News*, and *A.T. Journeys*.

Doug received the inaugural Environmental Service Award by Paddle Florida in 2015 "for conspicuous commitment, unflagging dedication and love of Florida's natural environment." For several years, he coordinated Florida's designated paddling trail system and helped to establish the 1,515-mile Florida Circumnavigational Saltwater Paddling Trail. He is currently the Outreach and Advocacy Director for Apalachicola Riverkeeper.

For more information, visit www.dougalderson.net.

The rivers flow not past, but through us, thrilling, tingling, vibrating every fiber and cell of the substance of our bodies, making them glide and sing.

—JOHN MUIR